CONTENTS

Your guide to the best players, biggest legends, top competitions and winners of all the major football events on the planet.

Statistics are correct until the end of the 2013-14 season, except where indicated. Where figures are disputed we have relied on clubs and historians for guidance.

Published 2014. Pedigree Books Limited, Beech Hill House, Walnut Gardens, Exeter, Devon, EX4 4DH.
www.pedigreebooks.com - books@pedigreegroup.co.uk
The Pedigree trademark, email and website addresses, are the sole and exclusive properties of Pedigree Group Limited, used under licence in this publication.

This is Football

The beautiful game's beautiful journey

Football has a long and fascinating history. It was believed the Ancient Greeks and Romans played the first form of football over 2,300 years ago. However, the game's world governing body, FIFA, recognises Cuju, a Chinese ball game played in the third Century BC, as the earliest form of the game.

Many other versions were played and adapted around the world in the thousands of years since, but it wasn't until the England Rugby Football and Association Football split in 1863 that the beautiful game's first official governing body was formed. Football was officially born.

This led to the formation of many clubs, the first being Notts County in England, who were actually founded a year prior to the FA, in which time they played a game similar to association football.

Although there were no official rules prior to the FA, some of the earliest regulations can be traced back to Japan and Korea.

The birth of England's governing body, which celebrated its 150th anniversary in 2013, led to others being formed around the world, most notably FIFA in 1904, who are responsible for looking after the game on a global scale and host the biggest competition in the sport - the World Cup - which was first held in 1930.

This summer's competition in Brazil will be all over the television which, like haircuts and shorts, has seen a drastic change since broadcasting the sport for the first time on September 16th 1937 when Arsenal took on Arsenal reserves at Highbury.

Those sketchy black and white highlights have transformed into countless live matches in high definition being shown on a daily basis. And with matches on demand, mobile or online, it's virtually impossible to make it home from work without finding out the result.

Prior to the last match of the 2013-14 season, Barcelona announced that Lionel Messi had become the highest paid player in the world, earning approximately £336,000 per week after tax. This is a far cry from the £4 per week wage limit of 1901, Johnny Haynes becoming the first £100 per week player in 1961 or even Alan Shearer becoming the highest paid player on the planet with a £34,000 per week pay packet in 1996.

Transfer fees have also escalated to the extreme. Many were horrified to see Trevor Francis become the first £1m player when signing for Nottingham Forest in 1979. Roll on 34 years and a player was sold for 86times that amount when Gareth Bale moved from Tottenham to Real Madrid for £86m in 2013. There's now so much money in football due to increased competition for broadcasting rights, commercialisation and globalisation of the game, which in England came from the birth of the Premier League in 1992.

So much has happened since the first international football match was played between England and Scotland in 1872, and now you can check out the facts, figures and stats (accurate as of the end of season 2013-14) in this yearbook.

Some records may never be beaten, but you can never say never in football. That's what makes it the beautiful game.

English Leagues

The English Football League first started in 1888 and is the oldest in the world. Preston North End were the inagrual winners and many clubs have made history since. Liverpool are the most successful side having lifted the title 18 times, while Leicester City are the latest to have achieved success. Manchester United are the most successful club in the country with 20 league trophies, but 13 of these came in the Premier League, which started in 1992, after 22 Football League clubs split away to create England's current top flight division. The Premier League is now the biggest commercial league in the world, and one where players from home and abroad dream of plying their trade. League One (third tier) and League Two (fourth tier), as they are now known, sit below the Football League's top division, the Championship, and are the other two fully professional leagues on England's football ladder.

Premier League

Since it was established in 1992, the Premier League has grown to become the richest and most exciting league in the world.

England's top division had 22 founding members - the Division One clubs who had broken away from the Football League and the three promoted from the old Second Division (Blackburn Rovers, Middlesbrough and Ipswich Town) before being cut down to its current 20 participants in 1995-96.

Manchester United are the most successful side since the formation of the Premier League having won the title 13 times in 22 seasons.

Although the league as we know it now was formed in the early 1990s, Preston North End won the first ever top division title, which was contested by 12 clubs, way back in 1888-89, while Manchester City are the most recent winners.

2013-2014

Manchester City won their second title in three seasons in what was a thrilling year. Arsenal led the way for the majority of the campaign before Chelsea and Jose Mourinho seemed destined to be crowned champions. But Liverpool had other ideas and put together an 11-match winning streak to give them a great chance of finishing top of the pile for the first time since 1990. However, a home defeat to Chelsea let Manchester City back in and Manuel Pellegrini guided The Citizens to their fourth top flight title with a victory over West Ham United on the final day of the season.

At the bottom, Fulham, Cardiff and Norwich City were relegated in a season that saw all three change their manager at least once.

2013-2014

Stats:

C - Champions, CL - Champions League, EL - Europa League, R - Relegation

POS	TEAM	P	W	D	L	F	A	GD	PTS
1	Manchester City	38	27	5	6	102	37	65	86
2	Liverpool	38	26	6	6	101	50	51	84
3	Chelsea	38	25	7	6	71	27	44	82
4	Arsenal	38	24	7	7	68	41	27	79
5	Everton	38	21	9	8	61	39	22	72
6	Tottenham Hotspur	38	21	6	11	55	51	4	69
7	Manchester United	38	19	7	12	64	43	21	64
8	Southampton	38	15	11	12	54	46	8	56
9	Stoke City	38	13	11	14	45	52	-7	50
10	Newcastle United	38	15	4	19	43	59	-16	49
11	Crystal Palace	38	13	6	19	33	48	-15	45
12	Swansea City	38	11	9	18	54	54	0	42
13	West Ham United	38	11	7	20	40	51	-11	40
14	Sunderland	38	10	8	20	41	60	-19	38
15	Aston Villa	38	10	8	20	39	61	-22	38
16	Hull City	38	10	7	21	38	53	-15	37
17	West Bromwich Albion	38	7	15	16	43	59	-16	36
18	Norwich City	38	8	9	21	28	62	-34	33
19	Fulham	38	9	5	24	40	85	-45	32
20	Cardiff City	38	7	9	22	32	74	-42	30

Top scorer: Luis Suarez (Liverpool) - 31 **Most assists:** Steven Gerrard (Liverpool) - 14
Clean sheets (club): Chelsea - 19 **Clean sheets (player):** Petr Cech (Chelsea) - 16 **Most goals:** Manchester City - 102
Most goals against: Fulham - 85 **Most goals in a game:** Manchester City 6-3 Arsenal, Cardiff City 3-6 Liverpool
Biggest win: Manchester City 7-0 Norwich City **Biggest crowd:** Manchester United 4-1 Aston Villa - 75,368
Most yellows: Aston Villa - 78 **Most reds:** Sunderland - 7

All time Stats:

Most titles: Manchester United - (13) **Most points in a season:** Chelsea (2004-05) - 95
Fewest points: Derby County (2007-08) - 11
Most goals in a season (player): Andrew Cole (Newcastle United, 1993-94), Alan Shearer (Blackburn Rovers, 1994-95) -34
Most goals in a season (club): Chelsea (2009-10) - 103 **Fewest goals:** Derby County (2007-08) - 20
Most relegations: Crystal Palace - 4 **Most wins:** Chelsea - 29 (2004-05, 2005-06) **Fewest wins:** Derby County (2007-08) - 1
Most defeats: Ipswich Town (1994-95), Sunderland (2005-06), Derby County (2007-08) - 29
Fewest defeats: Arsenal (2003-04) - 0 **Biggest undefeated streak:** Arsenal - 49 games (May 7, 2003 - October 24, 2004)
Most consecutive wins: Arsenal - 14 (February 10, 2002 - August 24, 2002)
Top scorer: Alan Shearer (Blackburn Rovers and Newcastle United) - 260
Most assists: Ryan Giggs (Manchester United) - 131 **Most appearances:** Ryan Giggs (Manchester United) - 632
Most yellow cards: Lee Bowyer (Leeds United, Newcastle United, West Ham United, Birmingham City), Paul Scholes (Manchester United), Kevin Davies (Southampton, Blackburn Rovers, Bolton Wanderers) - 99
Most red cards: Richard Dunne (Everton, Manchester City and Aston Villa), Patrick Vieira (Arsenal), Duncan Ferguson (Everton and Newcastle United) - 8 **Biggest crowd:** Manchester United 4-1 Blackburn Rovers (March 31, 2007) - 76,098
Biggest win: Manchester United 9-0 Ipswich Town (March 4, 1995)
Most goals in a game: Portsmouth 7-4 Reading (September 29, 2007)
Longest managerial tenure: Sir Alex Ferguson (Manchester United) - 6452 days
Shortest Managerial tenure: Les Reed (Charlton Athletic) - 41 days
Oldest player: John Burridge (Manchester City) - 43 years and 162 days
Youngest player: Matthew Briggs (Fulham) - 16 years and 65 days

2014-2015 clubs

Roll of Honour

Football League
1889 Preston North End
1890 Preston North End
1891 Everton
1892 Sunderland

Division One
1893 Sunderland
1894 Aston Villa
1895 Sunderland
1896 Aston Villa
1897 Aston Villa
1898 Sheffield United
1899 Aston Villa
1900 Aston Villa
1901 Liverpool
1902 Sunderland
1903 The Wednesday
1904 The Wednesday
1905 Newcastle United
1906 Liverpool
1907 Newcastle United
1908 Manchester United
1909 Newcastle United
1910 Aston Villa
1911 Manchester United
1912 Blackburn Rovers
1913 Sunderland
1914 Blackburn Rovers
1915 Everton
1920 West Bromwich Albion
1921 Burnley
1922 Liverpool
1923 Liverpool
1924 Huddersfield Town
1925 Huddersfield Town
1926 Huddersfield Town
1927 Newcastle United
1928 Everton
1929 Sheffield Wednesday
1930 Sheffield Wednesday
1931 Arsenal
1932 Everton
1933 Arsenal
1934 Arsenal
1935 Arsenal

1992

1936	Sunderland
1937	Manchester City
1938	Arsenal
1939	Everton
1947	Liverpool
1948	Arsenal
1949	Portsmouth
1950	Portsmouth
1951	Tottenham
1952	Manchester United
1953	Arsenal
1954	Wolverhampton Wanderers
1955	Chelsea
1956	Manchester United
1957	Manchester United
1958	Wolverhampton Wanderers
1959	Wolverhampton Wanderers
1960	Burnley
1961	Tottenham
1962	Ipswich Town
1963	Everton
1964	Liverpool
1965	Manchester United
1966	Liverpool
1967	Manchester United
1968	Manchester City
1969	Leeds United
1970	Everton

1971	Arsenal
1972	Derby County
1973	Liverpool
1974	Leeds United
1975	Derby County
1976	Liverpool
1977	Liverpool
1978	Nottingham Forest
1979	Liverpool
1980	Liverpool
1981	Aston Villa
1982	Liverpool
1983	Liverpool
1984	Liverpool
1985	Everton
1986	Liverpool
1987	Everton
1988	Liverpool
1989	Arsenal
1990	Liverpool
1991	Arsenal
1992	Leeds United

Premier League

1993	Manchester United
1994	Manchester United
1995	Blackburn Rovers
1996	Manchester United
1997	Manchester United
1998	Arsenal
1999	Manchester United
2000	Manchester United
2001	Manchester United
2002	Arsenal
2003	Manchester United
2004	Arsenal
2005	Chelsea
2006	Chelsea
2007	Manchester United
2008	Manchester United
2009	Manchester United
2010	Chelsea
2011	Manchester United
2012	Manchester City
2013	Manchester United
2014	Manchester City

Championship

E nglish football's second tier has been in existence from 1892. It was originally known as Division Two before being renamed Division One when the Premier League was born. In 2004 the Football League decided to rebrand their three divisions resulting in the league becoming known as the Championship. Leicester City and Manchester City are the most successful clubs at this level having won the title on seven occasions.

Stats:

Top scorer: Ross McCormack (Leeds United) - 28
Most assists: Craig Conway (Blackburn Rovers) - 14
Clean sheets (club): Brighton - 20
Clean sheets (player): Tom Heaton (Burnley) - 19
Most goals: Derby County - 84
Most goals against: Barnsley - 77
Most goals in a game: Derby County 4-4 Ipswich Town, Leicester City 5-3 Bolton Wanderers, Reading 7-1 Bolton Wanderers
Biggest win: Reading 7-1 Bolton Wanderers, Sheffield Wednesday 6-0 Leeds United
Biggest crowd: Derby County 5-0 Nottingham Forest - 33,004
Most yellows: Watford - 99
Most reds: Blackpool - 10

2013-2014

Champions: Leicester City
Runners-up: Burnley
Play-off winners: Queens Park Rangers
Play-offs: Derby County, Queens Park Rangers, Wigan Athletic, Brighton & Hove Albion
Relegated: Doncaster, Barnsley, Yeovil Town

2014-2015 clubs

Birmingham City, Blackburn Rovers, Blackpool, Bolton Wanderers, Bournemouth, Brentford, Brighton & Hove Albion, Cardiff City, Charlton Athletic, Derby County, Fulham, Huddersfield Town, Ipswich Town, Leeds United, Middlesbrough, Millwall, Norwich City, Nottingham Forest, Reading, Rotherham United, Sheffield Wednesday, Watford, Wigan Athletic, Wolverhampton Wanderers

2013-2014

Roll of Honour

Division Two

1893	Small Heath
1894	Liverpool
1895	Bury
1896	Liverpool
1897	Notts County
1898	Burnley
1899	Manchester City
1900	The Wednesday
1901	Grimsby Town
1902	West Bromwich Albion
1903	Manchester City
1904	Preston North End
1905	Liverpool
1906	Bristol City
1907	Nottingham Forest
1908	Bradford City
1909	Bolton Wanderers
1910	Manchester City
1911	West Bromwich Albion
1912	Derby County
1913	Preston North End
1914	Notts County
1915	Derby County
1920	Tottenham
1921	Birmingham City
1922	Nottingham Forest
1923	Notts County
1924	Leeds United
1925	Leicester City
1926	Sheffield Wednesday
1927	Middlesbrough
1928	Manchester City
1929	Middlesbrough
1930	Blackpool
1931	Everton
1932	Wolverhampton Wanderers
1933	Stoke City
1934	Grimsby Town
1935	Brentford
1936	Manchester United
1937	Leicester City
1938	Aston Villa
1939	Blackburn Rovers
1947	Manchester City
1948	Birmingham City

1949	Fulham
1950	Tottenham
1951	Preston North End
1952	Sheffield Wednesday
1953	Sheffield United
1954	Leicester City
1955	Birmingham City
1956	Sheffield Wednesday
1957	Leicester City
1958	West Ham
1959	Sheffield Wednesday
1960	Aston Villa
1961	Ipswich Town
1962	Liverpool
1963	Stoke City
1964	Leeds United
1965	Newcastle United
1966	Manchester City
1967	Coventry City
1968	Ipswich Town
1969	Derby County
1970	Huddersfield Town
1971	Leicester City
1972	Norwich City
1973	Burnley
1974	Middlesbrough
1975	Manchester United
1976	Sunderland
1977	Wolverhampton Wanderers
1978	Bolton Wanderers
1979	Crystal Palace
1980	Leicester City
1981	West Ham
1982	Luton Town
1983	Queens Park Rangers
1984	Chelsea
1985	Oxford United
1986	Norwich City
1987	Derby County
1988	Millwall
1989	Chelsea
1990	Leeds United
1991	Oldham Athletic
1992	Ipswich Town

Division One

1993	Newcastle United
1994	Crystal Palace
1995	Middlesbrough
1996	Sunderland
1997	Bolton Wanderers
1998	Nottingham Forest
1999	Sunderland
2000	Charlton Athletic
2001	Fulham
2002	Manchester City
2003	Portsmouth
2004	Norwich City

Championship

2005	Sunderland
2006	Reading
2007	Sunderland
2008	West Bromwich Albion
2009	Wolverhampton Wanderers
2010	Newcastle United
2011	Queens Park Rangers
2012	Reading
2013	Cardiff City
2014	Leicester City

2010

League One

The third tier of English football was born in 1920, but just for one season before splitting into regional divisions, Division Three North and South. It stayed this way until 1958 when it reverted back to a national league. The division was renamed Division Two in 1992 and received its current name of League One in 2004. Doncaster Rovers and Plymouth Argyle both share a record four titles each at this level.

Stats:

Top scorer: Sam Baldock (Bristol City), Britt Assombalonga (Peterborough United) - 28
Most assists: Bakary Sako (Wolverhampton Wanderers) - 14
Clean sheets (club): Wolverhampton Wanderers - 25
Clean sheets (player): Carl Ikeme (Wolverhampton Wanderers) - 22
Most goals: Wolverhampton Wanderers - 89
Most goals against: Crewe Alexandra - 80
Most goals in a game: Wolverhampton Wanderers 6-4 Rotherham United
Biggest win: Rotherham United 6-0 Notts County
Biggest crowd: Wolverhampton Wanderers 6-4 Rotherham United - 30,110
Most yellows: Notts County - 88
Most reds: Peterborough United, Tranmere Rovers - 8

2013-2014

Champions: Wolverhampton Wanderers (record 103 points)
Runners-up: Brentford
Play-off winners: Rotherham United
Play-offs: Leyton Orient, Rotherham United, Preston North End, Peterborough United
Relegated: Tranmere Rovers, Carlisle United, Shrewsbury Town, Stevenage

2014-2015 clubs

Barnsley, Bradford City, Bristol City, Chesterfield, Colchester United, Coventry City, Crawley Town, Crewe Alexandra, Doncaster Rovers, Fleetwood Town, Gillingham, Leyton Orient, MK Dons, Notts County, Oldham Athletic, Peterborough, Port Vale, Preston North End, Rochdale, Scunthorpe United, Sheffield United, Swindon Town, Walsall, Yeovil Town

2013-2014

Roll of Honour

Third Division
1921 Crystal Palace

Third Division North/South
1922 Stockport County/ Southampton
1923 Nelson/ Bristol City
1924 Wolverhampton/ Portsmouth
1925 Darlington/ Swansea Town
1926 Grimsby Town/ Reading
1927 Stoke City/ Bristol City
1928 Bradford Park/ Avenue Millwall
1929 Bradford City/ Charlton Athletic
1930 Port Vale/ Plymouth Argyle
1931 Chesterfield/ Notts County
1932 Lincoln City/ Fulham
1933 Hull City/ Brentford
1934 Barnsley/ Norwich City
1935 Doncaster Rovers/ Charlton Athletic
1936 Chesterfield/ Coventry City
1937 Stockport County/ Luton Town
1938 Tranmere Rovers/ Millwall
1939 Barnsley/ Newport County
1947 Doncaster Rovers/ Cardiff City
1948 Lincoln City/ Queens Park Rangers
1949 Hull City/ Swansea Town
1950 Doncaster Rovers/ Notts County
1951 Rotherham United/ Nottingham Forest
1952 Lincoln City/ Plymouth Argyle
1953 Oldham Athletic/ Bristol Rovers
1954 Port Vale/ Ipswich Town
1955 Barnsley/ Bristol City
1956 Grimsby Town/ Leyton Orient
1957 Derby County/ Ipswich Town
1958 Scunthorpe United/ Brighton & Hove Albion

Third Division
1959 Plymouth Argyle
1960 Southampton
1961 Bury
1962 Portsmouth
1963 Northampton Town
1964 Coventry City
1965 Carlisle United
1966 Hull City
1967 Queens Park Rangers
1968 Oxford United
1969 Watford
1970 Leyton Orient
1971 Preston North End
1972 Aston Villa
1973 Bolton Wanderers
1974 Oldham Athletic
1975 Blackburn Rovers
1976 Hereford United
1977 Mansfield Town
1978 Wrexham
1979 Shrewsbury Town
1980 Grimsby Town
1981 Rotherham United
1982 Burnley
1983 Portsmouth
1984 Oxford United
1985 Bradford City
1986 Reading
1987 Bournemouth
1988 Sunderland
1989 Wolverhampton Wanderers

1990 Bristol Rovers
1991 Cambridge United
1992 Brentford
1993 Stoke City
1994 Reading
1995 Birmingham City
1996 Swindon Town
1997 Bury
1998 Watford
1999 Fulham
2000 Preston North End
2001 Millwall
2002 Brighton and Hove Albion
2003 Wigan Athletic
2004 Plymouth Argyle

League One
2005 Luton Town
2006 Southend United
2007 Scunthorpe United
2008 Swansea City
2009 Leicester City
2010 Norwich City
2011 Brighton and Hove Albion
2012 Charlton Athletic
2013 Doncaster Rovers
2014 Wolverhampton Wanderers

2006

League Two

The lowest division of English professional football, League Two was first born as Division Four in 1958 after the decision to merge Third Division North and South together. This became known as Division Three in 1992 before the Football League's rebrand saw it adopt its current name in 2004. Doncaster Rovers, Peterborough United and Chesterfield are the most successful clubs at this level having won the title on two occasions.

Stats:

Top scorer: Sam Winnall (Scunthorpe United) - 23
Most assists: Kevan Hurst (Southend United) - 13
Clean sheets (club): York City - 22
Clean sheets (player): Sam Slocombe (Scunthorpe United) - 21
Most goals: Chesterfield - 71
Most goals against: Portsmouth, Torquay United - 66
Most goals in a game:
Fleetwood Town 5-4 Mansfield Town
Biggest win: Plymouth Argyle 5-0 Morecambe
Biggest crowd:
Portsmouth 1-4 Oxford United - 18,181
Most yellows: Mansfield - 86
Most reds: Rochdale, Wycombe Wanderers - 9

2013-2014

Champions: Chesterfield
Runners-up: Scunthorpe United
Third place: Rochdale
Play-off winners: Fleetwood Town
Play-offs: Fleetwood Town, Southend United, Burton Albion, York City
Relegated: Bristol Rovers, Torquay United

2014-2015 clubs

Accrington Stanley, AFC Wimbledon, Burton Albion, Bury, Cambridge United, Carlisle United, Cheltenham Town, Dagenham & Redbridge, Exeter City, Hartlepool United, Luton Town, Mansfield Town, Morecambe, Newport County, Northampton Town, Oxford United, Plymouth Argyle, Portsmouth, Shrewsbury, Southend United, Stevenage, Tranmere Rovers, Wycombe Wanderers, York City

2013-2014

Roll of Honour

Fourth Division
1959 Port Vale
1960 Walsall
1961 Peterborough United
1962 Millwall
1963 Brentford
1964 Gillingham
1965 Brighton and Hove Albion
1966 Doncaster Rovers
1967 Stockport County
1968 Luton Town
1969 Doncaster Rovers
1970 Chesterfield
1971 Notts County
1972 Grimsby Town
1973 Southport
1974 Peterborough United
1975 Mansfield Town
1976 Lincoln City
1977 Cambridge United
1978 Watford
1979 Reading
1980 Huddersfield Town
1981 Southend United
1982 Sheffield United
1983 Wimbledon
1984 York City
1985 Chesterfield
1986 Swindon Town
1987 Northampton Town
1988 Wolverhampton Wanderers
1989 Rotherham United
1990 Exeter City
1991 Darlington
1992 Burnley

Third Division
1993 Cardiff City
1994 Shrewsbury Town
1995 Carlisle United
1996 Preston North End
1997 Wigan Athletic
1998 Notts County
1999 Brentford
2000 Swansea City
2001 Brighton and Hove Albion
2002 Plymouth Argyle
2003 Rushden and Diamonds
2004 Doncaster Rovers

League Two
2005 Yeovil Town
2006 Carlisle United
2007 Walsall
2008 MK Dons
2009 Brentford
2010 Notts County
2011 Chesterfield
2012 Swindon Town
2013 Gillingham
2014 Chesterfield

2012

Conference

The Conference Premier first started in 1979 and is the top tier in non-league football. It is the division where every side is scrpapping their hardest to reach the Football League and one that has been known as a graveyard for clubs relegated from the fourth tier. Prior to 1987, clubs in the Conference had to be elected in order to gain promotion to the Football League, but after that the champions and, from 2003, one play-off winner automatically moved up the football pyramid. Stevenage Borough, Barnet, Kidderminster Harriers, Macclesfield Town, Maidstone United, Enfield and Altrincham both hold a record two league titles at this level.

Stats:

Top scorer: Andre Gray (Luton Town), Lee Gregory (Halifax Town) - 30
Most assists: Sean Newton (Lincoln City) - 15
Clean sheets (club): Luton Town - 23
Clean sheets (player): Mark Tyler (Luton Town) - 23
Most goals: Luton Town - 102
Most goals against: Hyde - 119
Most goals in a game:
Cambridge United 7-2 Hyde
Biggest win: Forest Green Rovers 8-0 Hyde
Biggest crowd: Luton Town 4-1
Forest Green Rovers - 10,044
Most yellows: Chester City - 94
Most reds: Chester City - 11

2013-2014

Champions: Luton Town
Play-off winners: Cambridge United
Play-offs: Cambridge United, Gateshead, Grimsby Town, Halifax Town
Relegated: Chester, Dartford, Tamworth, Hyde

2014-2015 clubs

AFC Telford United, Aldershot Town, Alfreton Town, Altrincham, Barnet, Braintree Town, Bristol Rovers, Chester, Dartford, Dover Athletic, Eastleigh, FC Halifax Town, Forest Green Rovers, Gateshead, Grimsby Town, Kidderminster Harriers, Lincoln City, Macclesfield Town, Nuneaton Town, Southport, Torquay United, Welling United, Woking, Wrexham

2014

Conference Premier

1980	Altrincham	**1992**	Colchester United	**2004**	Chester City
1981	Altrincham	**1993**	Wycombe Wanderers	**2005**	Barnet
1982	Runcorn	**1994**	Kidderminster Harriers	**2006**	Accrington Stanley
1983	Enfield	**1995**	Macclesfield Town	**2007**	Dagenham & Redbridge
1984	Maidstone United	**1996**	Stevenage Borough	**2008**	Aldershot Town
1985	Wealdstone	**1997**	Macclesfield Town	**2009**	Burton Albion
1986	Enfield	**1998**	Halifax Town	**2010**	Stevenage Borough
1987	Scarborough	**1999**	Cheltenham Town	**2011**	Crawley Town
1988	Lincoln City	**2000**	Kidderminster Harriers	**2012**	Fleetwood Town
1989	Maidstone United	**2001**	Rushden & Diamonds	**2013**	Mansfield Town
1990	Darlington	**2002**	Boston United	**2014**	Luton Town
1991	Barnet	**2003**	Yeovil Town		

2013

Scottish Premiership

The Scottish League was established in 1890 and was renamed the First Division three years later when a second tier was introduced. It stayed this way until 1975 when it became known as the Premier Division due to the birth of a Third Division. Clubs in the top tier then decided to follow England's example and split from the Scottish Football League, creating the Scottish Premier League (SPL) in1998. But this folded in 2013 after the Scottish Premier League and Scottish Football League merged to create the Scottish Professional Football League, leading to the country's top division now being known as the Scottish Premiership. Rangers are the most successful club having won the title 54 times.

2013-2014

Champions: Celtic
Runners-up: Motherwell
Relegated: Heart of Midlothian, Hibernian

2014-2015 clubs

Aberdeen, Celtic, Dundee, Dundee United, Hamilton Academical, Inverness Caledonian Thistle, Kilmarnock, Motherwell, Partick Thistle, Ross County, St. Johnstone, St. Mirren

2013-2014

Stats:

Top scorer: Kris Commons (Celtic) - 23
Most assists: Kallum Higginbotham (Partick Thistle) - 12
Clean sheets (club): Celtic - 21
Clean sheets (player):
Fraser Forster (Celtic) - 21
Most goals: Celtic - 102
Most goals against: Heart of Midlothian, Kilmarnock - 65
Most goals in a game:
Kilmarnock 2-5 Celtic,
St. Mirren 4-3 St. Johnstone,
Inverness Caledonian Thistle 3-4 Aberdeen,
Motherwell 4-3 Partick Thistle
Biggest win:
Celtic 6-0 Inverness Caledonian Thistle
Biggest crowd:
Celtic 1-0 Partick Thistle - 52,670
Most yellows: Heart of Midlothian, Ross County, Partick Thistle - 70
Most reds: Heart of Midlothian, Ross County, Partick Thistle, Hibernian, St. Johnstone, Kilmarnock - 5

Roll of Honour

Scottish League
1891 Dumbarton and Rangers
1892 Dumbarton
1893 Celtic

First Division
1894 Celtic
1895 Heart of Midlothian
1896 Celtic
1897 Heart of Midlothian
1898 Celtic
1899 Rangers
1900 Rangers
1901 Rangers
1902 Rangers
1903 Hibernian
1904 Third Lanark
1905 Celtic
1906 Celtic
1907 Celtic
1908 Celtic
1909 Celtic
1910 Celtic
1911 Rangers
1912 Rangers
1913 Rangers
1914 Celtic
1915 Celtic
1916 Celtic
1917 Celtic
1918 Rangers
1919 Celtic
1920 Rangers
1921 Rangers
1922 Celtic
1923 Rangers
1924 Rangers
1925 Rangers
1926 Celtic
1927 Rangers
1928 Rangers
1929 Rangers
1930 Rangers
1931 Rangers
1932 Motherwell
1933 Rangers
1934 Rangers
1935 Rangers
1936 Celtic
1937 Rangers
1938 Celtic
1939 Rangers
1947 Rangers
1948 Hibernian
1949 Rangers
1950 Rangers
1951 Hibernian
1952 Hibernian
1953 Rangers
1954 Celtic
1955 Aberdeen
1956 Rangers
1957 Rangers
1958 Heart of Midlothian
1959 Rangers
1960 Heart of Midlothian
1961 Rangers
1962 Dundee
1963 Rangers
1964 Rangers
1965 Kilmarnock
1966 Celtic
1967 Celtic
1968 Celtic
1969 Celtic
1970 Celtic
1971 Celtic
1972 Celtic
1973 Celtic
1974 Celtic
1975 Rangers

Premier Division
1976 Rangers
1977 Celtic
1978 Rangers
1979 Celtic
1980 Aberdeen
1981 Celtic
1982 Celtic
1983 Dundee United
1984 Aberdeen
1985 Aberdeen
1986 Celtic
1987 Rangers
1988 Celtic
1989 Rangers
1990 Rangers
1991 Rangers
1992 Rangers
1993 Rangers
1994 Rangers
1995 Rangers
1996 Rangers
1997 Rangers
1998 Celtic

Premier League
1999 Rangers
2000 Rangers
2001 Celtic
2002 Celtic
2003 Rangers
2004 Celtic
2005 Rangers
2006 Celtic
2007 Celtic
2008 Celtic
2009 Rangers
2010 Rangers
2011 Rangers
2012 Celtic
2013 Celtic

Premiership
2014 Celtic

All time stats:
Most titles: Rangers - 54
Most appearances: Celtic - 117
Most goals: Willie MacFadyen (Motherwell, 1931-32) - 52
Fewest defeats: Celtic (1897-98), Rangers (1898-99) - 0
Biggest undefeated streak: Celtic - 62 games (November 20, 1915 - April 21, 1917)
Most consecutive wins: Celtic - 25 (2003-04)
Top scorer: Jimmy McGrory (Celtic and Clydebank) - 410
Most appearances: Bob Ferrier (Motherwell) - 626
Biggest crowd: Rangers 2-1 Celtic (January 2, 1939) - 118,567
Biggest win: Celtic 11-0 Dundee (October 26, 1895)

Rest of Scotland

The rest of the Scottish football pyramid has been through numerous alterations over the years. The second tier has changed name on four occasions before being rebranded as the Championship in 2013, while the third tier is even more complicated having been split into north and south sections for a six-year period in the early 1950s. A fourth division wasn't introduced until 1994, as part of a restructuring process to allow Ross County and Inverness Caledonian Thistle into the Football League system.

2013-14
Championship
Champions: Dundee
Promoted: Hamilton
Relegated: Morton
Top scorer: Rory Loy
(Falkirk) - 20
All-time
Most wins:
Falfirk,
St Johnstone - 7

2013-14
League 1
Champions: Rangers
Relegated: Arbroath, East Fife
Top scorer: Michael Moffat (Ayr United) - 26
All-time **Most wins:**
Stirling Albion - 5

2013-14
League 2
Champions: Peterhead
Promoted: Stirling Albion
Top scorer: Rory McAllister (Peterhead) - 32
All-time **Most wins:**
Livingstone, Alloa Athletic -2

UK and Ireland

W ales and Northern Ireland, the two other countries that make up the United Kingdom, and the Republic of Ireland also play host to top flight football.

Joe Gormley, Cliftonville

2013-14
Welsh Premier League
Champions: The New Saints
Runners-up:
Airbus UK Broughton
Play-off winner: Bangor City
Relegated: Afan Lido
Top scorer: Chris Venables
(Aberystwyth Town) - 24

All-time
Most wins:
The New Saints - 8
Top scorer: Marc Lloyd
Williams (Porthmadog,
Bangor City, Aberystwyth
Town, Total Network
Solution, Rhyl,
Newtown, Airbus UK
Broughton) - 319

2013-14
NIFL Premiership
Champions: Cliftonville
Runners-up: Linfield
Relegated: Ards
Top scorer: Joe Gormley (Cliftonville) - 27

All-time **Most wins:** Linfield - 51
Top scorer: Jimmy Jones (Belfast Celtic,
Glenavon, Portadown, Bangor) - 332

2013
League of Ireland
Champions: St Patrick's
Runners-up: Dundalk
Relegated: Shelbourne
Top scorer: David O'Sullivan (Longford Town) - 21

All-time **Most wins:** Shamrock Rovers - 17
Top scorer: Brendan Bradley (Derry City, Finn
Harps, Athlone Town, Sligo Rovers) - 235

FA Cup

The FA Cup first started in 1871, making it the oldest association competition in world football. Teams from the Premier League all the way down to the county leagues compete in the tournament. This has seen many giant-killings over the years, where the bigger clubs have been knocked out by those lower down the pyramid. The final, which if drawn used to be replayed until 1994 when extra-time and penalties were implemented, was held at various locations until moving to Wembley Stadium in 1923, where it remained for 77 years until the rebuilding of England's most iconic ground began in 2000. This saw the match moved to Cardiff's Millennium Stadium for six years until the new Wembley hosted its first final in 2007. Premier League and Championship teams don't enter the draw until the Third Round, by which time only a minority of the non-league sides would've made it through the qualifying and first two rounds. Manchester United and Arsenal have lifted the trophy, which has had a number of sponsors from Littlewoods Pools to Budweiser, a joint-record 11 times.

2013-2014

Arsenal ended a nine-year wait for a trophy by coming from 2-0 down to beat Hull City 3-2 at Wembley Stadium. James Chester and Curtis Davies had put Steve Bruce's Tigers ahead in a dream opening eight minutes for the Yorkshire side. But a Santi Cazorla free-kick and Laurent Koscielny's equaliser took the game into extra-time, where Aaron Ramsey struck the winner for the Gunners.

2013-2014

Roll of Honour

1872	Wanderers
1873	Wanderers
1874	Oxford University
1875	Royal Engineers
1876	Wanderers
1877	Wanderers
1878	Wanderers
1879	Old Etonians
1880	Clapham Rovers
1881	Old Carthusians
1882	Old Etonians
1883	Blackburn Olympic
1884	Blackburn Rovers
1885	Blackburn Rovers
1886	Blackburn Rovers
1887	Aston Villa
1888	West Brom
1889	Preston North End
1890	Blackburn Rovers
1891	Blackburn Rovers
1892	West Bromwich Albion
1893	Wolverhampton Wanderers
1894	Notts County
1895	Aston Villa
1896	The Wednesday
1897	Aston Villa
1898	Nottingham Forest
1899	Sheffield United
1900	Bury
1901	Tottenham Hotspur
1902	Sheffield United
1903	Bury
1904	Manchester City
1905	Aston Villa
1906	Everton
1907	The Wednesday
1908	Wolverhampton Wanderers
1909	Manchester United
1910	Newcastle United
1911	Bradford City
1912	Barnsley
1913	Aston Villa 1 Sunderland 0
1914	Burnley
1915	Sheffield United
1920	Aston Villa
1921	Tottenham Hotspur
1922	Huddersfield Town

1923

1923	Bolton Wanderers
1924	Newcastle United
1925	Sheffield United
1926	Bolton Wanderers
1927	Cardiff City
1928	Blackburn Rovers
1929	Bolton Wanderers
1930	Arsenal
1931	West Bromwich Albion

Stats:

Winners: Arsenal
Runners-up: Hull City
Top scorer: Britt Assombalonga (Peterborough United), Sam Clucas (Mansfield Town), Joe Garner (Preston North End) - 5
Most assists: Lee Holmes (Preston North End) - 8
Clean sheets (club): Peterborough United, Preston North End - 3
Clean sheets (player): Robert Olejnik (Peterborough United), Declan Rudd (Preston North End) - 3
Most goals: Arsenal - 16
Most goals against: Sheffield United - 10
Most goals in a game:
St. Albans City 1-8 Mansfield Town
Biggest win: St. Albans City 1-8 Mansfield Town
Biggest crowd: Arsenal 3-2 Hull City (Wembley final) - 89,345

1960

1932	Newcastle United	**1963**	Manchester United
1933	Everton	**1964**	West Ham United
1934	Manchester City	**1965**	Liverpool
1935	Sheffield Wednesday	**1966**	Everton
1936	Arsenal	**1967**	Tottenham Hotspur
1937	Sunderland	**1968**	West Bromwich Albion
1938	Preston North End	**1969**	Manchester City
1939	Portsmouth	**1970**	Chelsea
1946	Derby County	**1971**	Arsenal
1947	Charlton Athletic	**1972**	Leeds United
1948	Manchester United	**1973**	Sunderland
1949	Wolverhampton Wanderers	**1974**	Liverpool
1950	Arsenal	**1975**	West Ham United
1951	Newcastle United	**1976**	Southampton
1952	Newcastle United	**1977**	Manchester United
1953	Blackpool	**1978**	Ipswich Town
1954	West Bromwich Albion	**1979**	Arsenal
1955	Newcastle United	**1980**	West Ham United
1956	Manchester City	**1981**	Tottenham Hotspur
1957	Aston Villa	**1982**	Tottenham Hotspur
1958	Bolton Wanderers	**1983**	Manchester United
1959	Nottingham Forest	**1984**	Everton
1960	Wolverhampton Wanderers	**1985**	Manchester United
1961	Tottenham Hotspur	**1986**	Liverpool
1962	Tottenham Hotspur	**1987**	Coventry City

1988	Wimbledon
1989	Liverpool
1990	Manchester United
1991	Tottenham Hotspur
1992	Liverpool
1993	Arsenal
1994	Manchester United
1995	Everton
1996	Manchester United
1997	Chelsea
1998	Arsenal
1999	Manchester United
2000	Chelsea
2001	Liverpool
2002	Arsenal
2003	Arsenal
2004	Manchester United
2005	Arsenal
2006	Liverpool
2007	Chelsea
2008	Portsmouth
2009	Chelsea
2010	Chelsea
2011	Manchester City
2012	Chelsea
2013	Wigan Athletic
2014	Arsenal

1988

All time Stats:

Most wins: Arsenal, Manchester United - 11
Most final appearances: Arsenal, Manchester United - 18
Most final defeats: Everton - 8
Most winners' medals: Ashley Cole (Arsenal, Chelsea) - 7
Most final goals:
Ian Rush (Liverpool) - 5
Most final appearances:
Arthur Kinnaird
(Wanderers, Old Etonians) - 9
Biggest final win: Bury 6-0 Derby County
Most goals in a final: Blackburn Rovers 6-1 Sheffield Wednesday (1890),
Blackpool 4-3 Bolton Wanderers (1953)
Most goals in a season (player): Jimmy Ross - 19 (Preston North End, 1887-88)
Biggest undefeated streak: Blackburn Rovers - 22 games (1884-86)
Top scorer: Henry Cursham (Notts County) - 49
Biggest crowd: Bolton Wanderers 2-0 West Ham United (April 28, 1923) - 126,047
Biggest win: Preston North End 26-0 Hyde United (October 15, 1887)
Most goals in a game: Preston North End 26-0 Hyde United (October 15, 1887)
Oldest finalist: Billy Hampson (Newcastle United) - 41 years and 257 days
Youngest finalist: Curtis Weston (Millwall) - 17 years and 119 days

League Cup

The Football League Cup first started in 1960 and was devised as a way for clubs to make up lost revenue they would lose when the league was re-organised. It was and still is played as a midweek floodlit tournament. It is often referred to by the name of the competition's sponsor - the first being Milk Marketing Brand between 1982-1986 to its current backer, Capital One. The tournament, which saw drawn finals go to replays until 1998, was critisised for a long time, with many clubs and officials labelling it as an unwelcome distraction from major competions, leading to some even refusing to participate. However, a place in the Europa League, formerly the UEFA Cup, is awarded to the winner - something which now sees all 92 clubs take the honour more seriously. Liverpool are the most successful club having lifted the trophy a record eight times.

2013-2014

Manchester City won the tournament for a third time and first time since 1976 by beating Sunderland 3-1 at Wembley. The Black Cats, who were then struggling in the Premier League, took a first half lead through Fabio Borini. However, wondergoals from Yaya Toure and Samir Nasri tuened the match on its head. Jesus Navas' late strike sealed the victory for Manuel Pellegrini's side.

2013-2014

Stats:

Top scorer: Alvaro Negredo (Manchester City) - 5
Most assists: Chris Burke (Birmingham City), Danny Welbeck (Manchester United) - 4
Clean sheets (club): Manchester City - 4
Clean sheets (player): Costel Pantilimon (Manchester City) - 4
Most goals: Manchester City - 22
Most goals against:
West Ham United - 13
Most goals in a game:
Norwich 6-3 Bury
Biggest win:
Manchester City 6-0 West Ham United,
Peterborough 6-0 Reading
Biggest crowd:
Manchester City 3-1 Sunderland
(Wembley final) - 84,697
Most yellows:
Sunderland - 20
Most reds:
Birmingham City,
Burnley - 1

Roll of Honour

1961	Aston Villa	**1979**	Nottingham Forest	**1998**	Chelsea
1962	Norwich City	**1980**	Wolves	**1999**	Tottenham
1963	Birmingham City	**1981**	Liverpool	**2000**	Leicester City
1964	Leicester City	**1982**	Liverpool	**2001**	Liverpool
1965	Chelsea	**1983**	Liverpool	**2002**	Blackburn
1966	West Bromwich Albion	**1984**	Liverpool	**2003**	Liverpool
1967	Queens Park Rangers	**1985**	Norwich City	**2004**	Middlesbrough
1968	Leeds United	**1986**	Oxford United	**2005**	Chelsea
1969	Swindon Town	**1987**	Arsenal	**2006**	Manchester United
1970	Manchester City	**1988**	Luton Town	**2007**	Chelsea
1971	Tottenham Hotspur	**1989**	Nottingham Forest	**2008**	Tottenham
1972	Stoke City	**1990**	Nottingham Forest	**2009**	Manchester United
1973	Tottenham Hotspur	**1991**	Sheffield Wednesday	**2010**	Manchester United
1974	Wolverhampton Wanderers	**1992**	Manchester United	**2011**	Birmingham City
		1993	Arsenal	**2012**	Liverpool
1975	Aston Villa	**1994**	Aston Villa	**2013**	Swansea City
1976	Manchester City	**1995**	Liverpool	**2014**	Manchester City
1977	Aston Villa	**1996**	Aston Villa		
1978	Nottingham Forest	**1997**	Leicester City		

1987

All time stats:

Most titles: Liverpool - 8
Most final appearances: Liverpool - 11
Top scorer: Geoff Hurst (West Ham United, Stoke City), Ian Rush (Liverpool, Newcastle United) - 49
Biggest win: Liverpool 10-0 Fulham (September 23, 1986), West Ham United 10-0 Bury (October 25, 1983)
Most winners' medals: Ian Rush (Liverpool) - 5

Community Shield

T he FA Community shield is the curtain raiser for the English domestic football campaign.

The season opener, previously known as the English Charity Shield until 2002, has its name because all proceeds from the match are distributed to community-based initiatives and charities around the country.

Played at Wembley Stadium since 1974, the tie is contested between the previous season's Premier League champions and FA Cup winners. If a club has done a domestic double then the team that finished runners-up in the league participates.

This wasn't always the case, with the first match in 1908 seeing First Division champions Manchester United take on Southern League Champions Queens Park Rangers.

Draws previously resulted in the two clubs sharing the trophy for six months each, but in 1993 penalties were re-introduced to separate the two teams.

Manchester United, who were the inaugural winners, have lifted the shield on a record 20 occasions, most recently defeating Wigan Athletic 2-0 in August 2013 thanks to two goals from Robin van Persie.

2013

Roll of Honour

1908	Manchester United
1909	Newcastle United
1910	Brighton & Hove Albion
1911	Manchester United
1912	Blackburn Rovers
1913	Professionals
1920	West Brom Albion
1921	Tottenham Hotspur
1922	Huddersfield Town
1923	Professionals
1924	Professionals
1925	Amateurs
1926	Amateurs
1927	Cardiff City
1928	Everton
1929	Professionals
1930	Arsenal
1931	Arsenal
1932	Everton
1933	Arsenal
1934	Arsenal
1935	Sheffield Wednesday
1936	Sunderland
1937	Manchester City
1938	Arsenal
1948	Arsenal
1949	Portsmouth and Wolverhampton Wanderers
1950	England XI
1951	Tottenham Hotspur
1952	Manchester United
1953	Arsenal
1954	Wolverhampton Wanderers and West Bromwich Albion
1955	Chelsea
1956	Manchester United
1957	Manchester United
1958	Bolton Wanderers
1959	Wolverhampton Wanderers
1960	Burnley and Wolverhampton Wanderers
1961	Tottenham Hotspur
1962	Tottenham Hotspur
1963	Everton
1964	Liverpool and West Ham United
1965	Manchester United and Liverpool
1966	Liverpool

2004

1994	Manchester United
1995	Everton
1996	Manchester United
1997	Manchester United
1998	Arsenal
1999	Arsenal
2000	Chelsea
2001	Liverpool
2002	Arsenal
2003	Manchester United
2004	Arsenal
2005	Chelsea
2006	Liverpool
2007	Manchester United
2008	Manchester United
2009	Chelsea
2010	Manchester United
2011	Manchester United
2012	Manchester City
2013	Manchester United

1967	Manchester United and Tottenham Hotspur
1968	Manchester City
1969	Leeds United
1970	Everton
1971	Leicester City
1972	Manchester City
1973	Burnley
1974	Liverpool
1975	Derby County
1976	Liverpool
1977	Manchester United and Liverpool
1978	Nottingham Forest
1979	Liverpool
1980	Liverpool
1981	Aston Villa and Tottenham Hotspur
1982	Liverpool
1983	Manchester United
1984	Everton
1985	Everton
1986	Everton and Liverpool
1987	Everton
1988	Liverpool
1989	Liverpool
1990	Manchester United and Liverpool
1991	Arsenal and Tottenham Hotspur
1992	Leeds United
1993	Manchester United

1966

Stats:

Most wins: Manchester United - 20
Most defeats: Manchester United - 9
Most winners' medals:
Ryan Giggs (Manchester United) - 10 wins
Most successful manager:
Sir Alex Ferguson (Manchester United) - 11
Most goals in a game:
Manchester United 8-4 Swindon Town (1911)

Europe

The best clubs in England compete against the best of the continent in the Champions League, while those who fell just short compete in the Europa League. These competitions see clubs go down in the history books and have showcased the world's greatest players on a yearly basis.

Away from continental competitions, Europe has some fantastic football to offer in their domestic leagues. Historic divisions that contain some of the biggest, richest and most successful clubs go head-to-head on a yearly basis to see who will be their country's best. Spain's La Liga, Italy's Serie A, France's Ligue 1 and Germany's Bundesliga are just four of many that are full of history and action packed moments.

Champions League

E urope's most prestigious club competition was originally known as the European Cup when it first began in 1955. Sixteen teams participated in the inaugural competition which was won by Real Madrid, who are the tournament's most successful club having lifted the trophy on 10 occasions. In 1992 UEFA rebranded it the Champions League and expanded the format, which included a round-robin group stage. These changes allowed some countries to provide four teams to compete in a tournament that sees 76 clubs participate from the first qualifying round through to the final. In 2000 a second group phase was introduced before a Round of 16 replaced this in the 2003-04 season.

The final, which takes place at a neutral venue unless the host stadium's team reaches the last two, has to be won through a bidding process.

2013-2014

Real Madrid won their tenth European Cup as they defeated city rivals Atletico Madrid in Lisbon. Diego Godin looked like he'd secured Diego Simeone side's first European Cup, but a Sergio Ramos injury-time equaliser took the clash into extra-time where goals from Gareth Bale, Marcelo and Cristiano Ronaldo secured Los Blancos the Champions League trophy 12 years after their last success in the competition.

Stats:

Winners: Real Madrid
Runners-up: Atletico Madrid
Top scorer: Cristiano Ronaldo (Real Madrid) - 17
Most assists: Wayne Rooney (Manchester United) - 8
Clean sheets (club): Chelsea - 7
Clean sheets (player): Petr Cech (Chelsea), Iker Casillas (Real Madrid) - 6
Most goals: Real Madrid - 41
Most goals against: Anderlecht, Galatasaray, CSKA Moscow, Viktoria Plzen - 17
Most goals in a game: Barcelona 6-1 Celtic, Galatasaray 1-6 Real Madrid, Manchester City 5-2 CSKA Moscow
Biggest win: Bayern Munich 5-0 Viktoria Plzen, Barcelona 6-1 Celtic, Bayer Leverkusen 0-5 Manchester United, Galatasaray 1-6 Real Madrid, Anderlecht 0-5 Paris Saint-Germain
Biggest crowd: Barcelona 2-1 Manchester City - 85,957

2013-2014

Champions League Roll of Honour

1980

1977

European Cup

1956	Real Madrid
1957	Real Madrid
1958	Real Madrid
1959	Real Madrid
1960	Real Madrid
1961	Benfica
1962	Benfica
1963	AC Milan
1964	Inter Milan
1965	Inter Milan
1966	Real Madrid
1967	Celtic
1968	Manchester United
1969	AC Milan
1970	Feyenoord
1971	Ajax
1972	Ajax
1973	Ajax
1974	Bayern Munich
1975	Bayern Munich
1976	Bayern Munich
1977	Liverpool
1978	Liverpool
1979	Nottingham Forest

1987

1989	AC Milan
1990	AC Milan
1991	Red Star Belgrade
1992	Barcelona

Champions League

1993	Marseille
1994	AC Milan
1995	Ajax
1996	Juventus
1997	Borussia Dortmund
1998	Real Madrid
1999	Manchester United
2000	Real Madrid
2001	Bayern Munich
2002	Real Madrid
2003	AC Milan
2004	Porto
2005	Liverpool
2006	Barcelona
2007	AC Milan
2008	Manchester United
2009	Barcelona
2010	Inter Milan
2011	Barcelona
2012	Chelsea
2013	Bayern Munich
2014	Real Madrid

1980	Nottingham Forest
1981	Liverpool
1982	Aston Villa
1983	Hamburg
1984	Liverpool
1985	Juventus
1986	Steaua Bucharest
1987	Porto
1988	PSV Eindhoven

All time Stats:

Most wins: Real Madrid - 10
Most final appearances: Real Madrid - 13
Most final defeats: Bayern Munich, Benfica, Juventus - 5
Most winners' medals: Franciso Gento (Real Madrid) - 6
Most final goals: Ferenc Puskas, Alfredo Di Stefano (both Real Madrid) - 7
Most final appearances: Franciso Gento (Real Madrid), Paolo Maldini (AC Milan) - 8
Biggest final win: Real Madrid 7-3 Eintracht Frankfurt,
Bayern Munich 4-0 Atletico Madrid, AC Milan 4-0 Steaua Bucuresti, AC Milan 4-0 Barcelona
Most goals in a final: Real Madrid 7-3 Eintracht Frankfurt (1960)
Most goals in a season (player): Cristiano Ronaldo (Real Madrid, 2013-14) - 17
Biggest undefeated streak: Manchester United - 25 games (2007-09)
Top scorer: Raul (Real Madrid, Schalke 04) - 71
Biggest crowd: Celtic 2-1 Leeds United (April 15, 1970) - 136,505
Biggest win: Dinamo Bucuresti 11-0 Crusaders (October 3, 1973)
Biggest two-leg win: Benfica 18-0 Stade Dudelange
Most goals in a game: Feyenoord 12-2 KR Reykjavik (September 17, 1969)
Oldest finalist: Edwin van der Sar (Manchester United) - 40 years and 212 days
Youngest finalist: Antonio Simoes (Benfica) - 18 years and 129 days

Europa League

The younger brother of the Champions League was initially the Inter Cities Fairs Cup until UEFA took on the competition and renamed it the UEFA Cup in 1972. It was known by that name until Europe's governing body rebranded it the Europa League in 2009. Its current format, which sees 421 matches played from the first qualifying round in July up to the final in May, occurred after both the Cup Winners' Cup - in 1999 - and InterToto Cup - in 2009 - were merged into this marathon of a competition. Because it is viewed as a hindrance by some clubs due to the number of matches, UEFA will award the winner automatic qualification to the Champions League from the 2014-15 season. Twenty-seven clubs have lifted the trophy since its birth in 1971 with Juventus, Internazionale, Liverpool and 2014 winners Sevilla having been victorious a record three times since UEFA took control 43 years ago.

2013-2014

Sevilla won the competition for a third time in eight years after a dramatic penalty shoot-out victory over Benfica. With the scores goalless after 120 minutes, the Spanish side's goalkeeper Beto saved penalties from Oscar Cardoza and Rodrigo, allowing Kevin Gameiro to smash home the winning kick as Unai Emery's side held their nerve to win 4-2. The defeat condemned Benfica to an eighth European final defeat in a row since beating Real Madrid for the 1962 European Cup. It was also Jorge Jesus side's second Europa League final defeat in two years and one that ended their chance of claiming a historic quadruple.

2013-2014

Stats:

Top scorer: Jonatan Soriano
(FC Red Bull Salzburg) - 8
Most assists: Bibras Natkho (Rubin Kazan),
Kevin Kampl (Red Bull Salzburg) - 5
Clean sheets (club): AZ Alkmaar - 6
Clean sheets (player): Esteban Alvarado
(AZ Alkmaar) - 6
Most goals: Valencia - 26
Most goals against: NK Maribor - 16
Most goals in a game:
Maribor 2-5 Rubin Kazan
Biggest win: Basel 0-5 Valencia (a.e.t)
Biggest crowd:
Benfica 2-1 Juventus - 55,779
Most yellows: Sevilla - 37
Most reds: Freiburg - 4

Roll of Honour

Inter Cities Fairs Cup

1958	Barcelona
1960	Barcelona
1961	Roma
1962	Valencia
1963	Valencia
1964	Real Zaragoza
1965	Ferencvaros
1966	Barcelona
1967	Dinamo Zagreb
1968	Leeds United
1969	Newcastle United
1970	Arsenal
1971	Leeds United

UEFA Cup

1972	Tottenham Hotspur
1973	Liverpool
1974	Feyenoord
1975	Borussia Mönchengladbach
1976	Liverpool
1977	Juventus
1978	PSV
1979	Borussia Mönchengladbach
1980	Eintracht Frankfurt
1981	Ipswich Town
1982	IFK Göteborg
1983	Anderlecht
1984	Tottenham Hotspur
1985	Real Madrid
1986	Real Madrid
1987	IFK Göteborg
1988	Bayer Leverkusen
1989	Napoli
1990	Juventus
1991	Internazionale
1992	Ajax
1993	Juventus
1994	Internazionale
1995	Parma
1996	Bayern München
1997	Schalke 04
1998	Internazionale
1999	Parma
1900	Galatasaray
2001	Liverpool
2002	Feyenoord
2003	Porto
2004	Valencia
2005	CSKA Moskva
2006	Sevilla
2007	Sevilla
2008	Zenit Sankt-Peterburg
2009	Shakhtar Donetsk

Europa League

2010	Atlético Madrid
2011	FC Porto
2012	Atlético Madrid
2013	Chelsea
2014	Sevilla

All time stats:

Most titles: Juventus, Liverpool, Internazional, Sevilla - (3)
Most wins: Chelsea - 29 (2004-05, 2005-06)
Biggest undefeated streak: Arsenal - 49 games (May 7, 2003 - October 24, 2004)
Most consecutive wins: Atletico Madrid - 15 (2011-13)
Top scorer: Henrik Larsson (Feyenoord, Celtic, Helsingborgs) - 12
Most appearances: Giuseppe Bergomi (Internazionale) - 96
Biggest crowd: Manchester United 4-1 Blackburn Rovers (March 31, 2007) - 76,098
Biggest win: Ajax 14-0 Red Boys Differdange (October 3, 1984)
Biggest aggregate win: Feyenoord 21-0 Rumelange (September, 1972)
Most goals in a game: Ajax 14-0 Red Boys Differdange (October 3, 1984)
Oldest player: Brad Friedel (Tottenham Hotspur) - 42 years, 10 months and 2 days
Youngest player: Darko Velkovski (Rabotnicki Skopje) - 16 years, 1 month and 27 days

1973

La Liga

T he top division in Spain was founded in 1929, two years after José María Acha, a director at Arenas Club de Getxo, first came up with the idea of a national league. Real Madrid are the country's most successful side with 32 titles to their name.

2013-2014 stats
Champions: Atletico Madrid
Runners-up: Barcelona
Relegated: Osasuna, Real Valladolid, Real Betis
Top scorer: Cristiano Ronaldo (Real Madrid) - 31
Most assists: Angel di Maria (Real Madrid) - 17

All time:
Most titles: Real Madrid - 32
Most goals: Telmo Zarra (Athletic Bilbao) - 251
Most appearances: Andoni Zubizarreta
(Athletic Bilbao, Barcelona, Valencia) - 622

2013-2014

Roll of Honour

1929	Barcelona	**1960**	Barcelona	**1988**	Real Madrid
1930	Athletic Bilbao	**1961**	Real Madrid	**1989**	Real Madrid
1931	Athletic Bilbao	**1962**	Real Madrid	**1990**	Real Madrid
1932	Real Madrid	**1963**	Real Madrid	**1991**	Barcelona
1933	Real Madrid	**1964**	Real Madrid	**1992**	Barcelona
1934	Athletic Bilbao	**1965**	Real Madrid	**1993**	Barcelona
1935	Real Betis	**1966**	Atletico Madrid	**1994**	Barcelona
1936	Athletic Bilbao	**1967**	Real Madrid	**1995**	Real Madrd
1940	Atletico Aviacion	**1968**	Real Madrid	**1996**	Atletico Madrid
1941	Atletico Aviacion	**1969**	Real Madrid	**1997**	Real Madrid
1942	Valencia	**1970**	Atletico Madrid	**1998**	Barcelona
1943	Athletic Bilbao	**1971**	Valencia	**1999**	Barcelona
1944	Valencia	**1972**	Real Madrid	**2000**	Deportivo La Coruna
1945	Barcelona	**1973**	Atletico Madrid	**2001**	Real Madrid
1946	Sevilla	**1974**	Barcelona	**2002**	Valencia
1947	Valencia	**1975**	Real Madrid	**2003**	Real Madrid
1948	Barcelona	**1976**	Real Madrid	**2004**	Valencia
1949	Barcelona	**1977**	Atletico Madrid	**2005**	Barcelona
1950	Atletico Madrid	**1978**	Real Madrid	**2006**	Barcelona
1951	Atletico Madrid	**1979**	Real Madrid	**2007**	Real Madrid
1952	Barcelona	**1980**	Real Madrid	**2008**	Real Madrid
1953	Barcelona	**1981**	Real Sociedad	**2009**	Barcelona
1954	Real Madrid	**1982**	Real Sociedad	**2010**	Barcelona
1955	Real Madrid	**1983**	Athletic Bilbao	**2011**	Barcelona
1956	Athletic Bilbao	**1984**	Athletic Bilbao	**2012**	Real Madrid
1957	Real Madrid	**1985**	Barcelona	**2013**	Barcelona
1958	Real Madrid	**1986**	Real Madrid	**2014**	Atletico Madrid
1959	Barcelona	**1987**	Real Madrid		

Serie A

Italy's top tier is renowned for turning out world class teams having produced the most European Cup finalists. The league was officially formed in 1898 but was played in various regional groups until turning national in 1929. Juventus, who are the most recent champions, have lifted the title a record 30 times.

2013-2014 stats

Champions: Juventus **Runners-up:** AS Roma
Relegated: Livorno, Bologna, Catania
Top scorer: Circo Immobile (Torino) - 22
Most assists: Alessio Cerci (Torino) - 10

All time:

Most titles: Juventus - 30 **Most goals:** Silvio Piola
(Pro Vercelli, Lazio, Juventus, Novara) - 274
Most appearances: Paolo Maldini (AC Milan) - 647

2013-2014

Roll of Honour

Prima Categoria

1898	Genoa
1899	Genoa
1900	Genoa
1901	AC Milan
1902	Genoa
1903	Genoa
1904	Genoa
1905	Juventus
1906	AC Milan
1907	AC Milan
1908	Pro Vercelli
1909	Pro Vercelli
1910	Inter Milan
1911	Pro Vercelli
1912	Pro Vercelli
1913	Pro Vercelli
1914	Casale
1915	Genoa
1920	Inter Milan
1921	Pro Vercelli
1922	Novese

Prima Divisione

1922	Pro Vercelli
1923	Genoa
1924	Genoa
1925	Bologna
1926	Juventus

Divisione Nazionale

1927	Not awarded
1928	Torino
1929	Bologna

Serie A

1930	Inter Milan
1931	Juventus
1932	Juventus
1933	Juventus
1934	Juventus
1935	Juventus
1936	Bologna
1937	Bologna
1938	Inter Milan
1939	Bologna
1940	Inter Milan
1941	Bologna
1942	Roma
1943	Torino
1946	Torino
1947	Torino
1948	Torino
1949	Torino
1950	Juventus
1951	AC Milan
1952	Juventus
1953	Inter Milan
1954	Inter Milan
1955	AC Milan

1956	Fiorentina
1957	AC Milan
1958	Juventus
1959	AC Milan
1960	Juventus
1961	Juventus
1962	AC Milan
1963	Inter Milan
1964	Bologna
1965	Inter Milan
1966	Inter Milan
1967	Juventus
1968	AC Milan
1969	Fiorentina
1970	Cagliari Calcio
1971	Inter Milan
1972	Juventus
1973	Juventus
1974	Lazio
1975	Juventus
1976	Torino
1977	Juventus
1978	Juventus
1979	AC Milan
1980	Inter Milan
1981	Juventus
1982	Juventus
1983	Romas
1984	Juventus
1985	Verona

1986	Juventus
1987	Napoli
1988	AC Milan
1989	Inter Milan
1990	Napoli
1991	Sampdoria
1992	AC Milan
1993	AC Milan
1994	AC Milan
1995	Juventus
1996	AC Milan
1997	Juventus
1998	Juventus
1999	AC Milan
2000	Lazio
2001	Roma
2002	Juventus
2003	Juventus
2004	AC Milan
2005	Not awarded
2006	Inter Milan
2007	Inter Milan
2008	Inter Milan
2009	Inter Milan
2010	Inter Milan
2011	AC Milan
2012	Juventus
2013	Juventus
2014	Juventus

Bundesliga

Germany's top division is a relatively young league having only started in 1963. Bayern Munich are the most successful side with 23 titles to their name.

2013-2014 stats

Champions: Bayern Munich
Runners-up: Borussia Dortmund
Relegated: Nurnberg, Eintracht Braunschweig
Top scorer: Robert Lewandowski (Borussia Dortmund) - 20
Most assists: Marco Reus (Borussia Dortmund) - 13

All time:

Most titles: Bayern Munich - 23
Most goals: Gerd Muller (Bayern Munich) - 365
Most appearances:
Karl-Heinz Korbel (Eintracht Frankfurt) - 602

2013-2014

Roll of Honour

Year	Club	Year	Club	Year	Club
1964	Cologne	1978	Cologne	1998	Kaiserslautern
1965	Werder Bremen	1979	Hamburg	1999	Bayern Munich
1966	Munich 1860	1980	Bayern Munich	2000	Bayern Munich
1967	Eintracht Braunschweig	1981	Bayern Munich	2001	Bayern Munich
		1982	Hamburg	2002	Borussia Dortmund
1968	Nuremberg	1983	Hamburg	2003	Bayern Munich
1969	Bayern Munich	1984	Stuttgart	2004	Werder Bremen
1970	Borussia Monchengladbach	1985	Bayern Munich	2005	Bayern Munich
		1986	Bayern Munich	2006	Bayern Munich
1971	Borussia Monchengladbach	1987	Bayern Munich	2007	Stuttgart
		1988	Werder Bremen	2008	Bayern Munich
1972	Bayern Munich	1989	Bayern Munich	2009	Wolfsburg
1973	Bayern Munich	1990	Bayern Munich	2010	Bayern Munich
1974	Bayern Munich	1991	Kaiserslautern	2011	Borussia Dortmund
1975	Borussia Monchengladbach	1992	Stuttgart	2012	Borussia Dortmund
		1993	Werder Bremen	2013	Bayern Munich
1976	Borussia Monchengladbach	1994	Bayern Munich	2014	Bayern Munich
		1995	Borussia Dortmund		
1977	Borussia Monchengladbach	1996	Borussia Dortmund		
		1997	Bayern Munich		

Ligue 1

The top division in France was known as the National in its first season before becoming Division One. It wasn't until 2002 that it adopted its current name of Ligue 1. Saint-Etienne have won a record 10 titles, one more than Marseille.

2013-2014 stats

Champions: Paris Saint-Germain
Runners-up: AS Monaco
Relegated: Sochaux, Valenciennes, Ajaccio
Top scorer: Zlatan Ibrahimovic (PSG) - 25
Most assists: James Rodriguez (AS Monaco) - 12

All time:

Most titles: Saint-Etienne - 10
Most goals: Delio Onnis (AS Monaco) - 365
Most appearances: Mickaël Landreau (Nantes, Paris Saint-Germain, Lille, Bastia) - 604

2013-2014

Roll of Honour

National

1933	Olympique Lillois

Division One

1934	Sete
1935	Sochaux
1936	RCF Paris
1937	Marseille
1938	Sochaux
1939	Sete
1946	Lille
1947	Roubaix-Tourcoing
1948	Marseille
1949	Stade Reims
1950	Bordeaux
1951	Nice
1952	Nice
1953	Stade Reims
1954	Lille
1955	Stade Reims
1956	Nice
1957	Saint-Etienne
1958	Stade Reims
1959	Nice
1960	Stade Reims
1961	Monaco
1962	Stade Reims
1963	Monaco
1964	Saint-Etienne
1965	Nantes
1966	Nantes
1967	Saint-Etienne
1968	Saint-Etienne
1969	Saint-Etienne
1970	Saint-Etienne
1971	Marseille
1972	Marseille
1973	Nantes
1974	Saint-Etienne
1975	Saint-Etienne
1976	Saint-Etienne
1977	Nantes
1978	Monaco
1979	Strasbourg
1980	Nantes
1981	Saint-Etienne
1982	Monaco
1983	Nantes
1984	Bordeaux
1985	Bordeaux
1986	Paris Saint German
1987	Bordeaux
1988	Monaco
1989	Marseille
1990	Marseille
1991	Marseille
1992	Marseille
1993	unattributed
1994	Paris Saint German
1995	Nantes
1996	Auxerre
1997	Monaco
1998	Lens
1999	Bordeaux
2000	Monaco
2001	Nantes
2002	Lyon

Ligue 1

2003	Lyon
2004	Lyon
2005	Lyon
2006	Lyon
2007	Lyon
2008	Lyon
2009	Bordeaux
2010	Marseille
2011	Lille
2012	Montpellier
2013	Paris Saint-Germain
2014	Paris Saint-Germain

Eredivisie

Holland's top tier was founded in 1956, two years after professional football was born in the country. Ajax, who are just one of three clubs never to have been relegated from the league, are also the most successful having been crowned kings of the Netherlands 25 times.

2013-2014 stats

Champions: Ajax
Runners-up: Feyenoord
Relegated: RKC Waalwijk, NEC, Roda JC
Top scorer: Alfred Finnbogason (SC Heerenveen) - 29
Most assists: Dusan Tadic (FC Twente) - 14

All time:

Most titles: Ajax - 25
Most goals: Willy van der Kuijlen
(PSV Eindhoven, MVV Maastricht) - 311
Most appearances: Pim Doesburg (Sparta
Rotterdam, PSV Eindhoven) - 687

2013-2014

Roll of Honour

Year	Club	Year	Club	Year	Club
1957	Ajax	**1977**	Ajax	**1997**	PSV Eindhoven
1958	DOS	**1978**	PSV Eindhoven	**1998**	Ajax
1959	Sparta	**1979**	Ajax	**1999**	Feyenoord
1960	Ajax	**1980**	Ajax	**2000**	PSV Eindhoven
1961	Feyenoord	**1981**	AZ 67	**2001**	PSV Eindhoven
1962	Feyenoord	**1982**	Ajax	**2002**	Ajax
1963	PSV Eindhoven	**1983**	Ajax	**2003**	PSV Eindhoven
1964	DWS	**1984**	Feyenoord	**2004**	Ajax
1965	Feyenoord	**1985**	Ajax	**2005**	PSV Eindhoven
1966	Ajax	**1986**	PSV Eindhoven	**2006**	PSV Eindhoven
1967	Ajax	**1987**	PSV Eindhoven	**2007**	PSV Eindhoven
1968	Ajax	**1988**	PSV Eindhoven	**2008**	PSV Eindhoven
1969	Feyenoord	**1989**	PSV Eindhoven	**2009**	AZ
1970	Ajax	**1990**	Ajax	**2010**	Twente
1971	Feyenoord	**1991**	PSV Eindhoven	**2011**	Ajax
1972	Ajax	**1992**	PSV Eindhoven	**2012**	Ajax
1973	Ajax	**1993**	Feyenoord	**2013**	Ajax
1974	Feyenoord	**1994**	Ajax	**2014**	Ajax
1975	PSV Eindhoven	**1995**	Ajax		
1976	PSV Eindhoven	**1996**	Ajax		

Rest of Europe

The best from the rest of the continent

A PFG
Country: Bulgaria
Founded: 1924
Most titles: CSKA Sofia - 31
2014 Champions:
Ludogorets Razgrad

Prva HNL
Country: Croatia
Founded: 1992
Most titles:
Dinamo Zagreb - 16
2014 Champions:
Dinamo Zagreb

Gambrinus Liga
Country: Czech Republic
Founded: 1993
Most titles:
Sparta Prague - 12
2014 Champions:
Sparta Prague

Superliga
Country: Denmark
Founded: 1991
Most titles:
FC Copenhagen - 10
2014 Champions:
AaB Fodbold

Veikkausliiga
Country: Finland
Founded: 1990
Most titles: HJK Helsinki - 26
2013 Champions:
HJK Helsinki

Superleague
Country: Greece
Founded: 1927
Most titles: Olympiacos - 41
2014 Champions:
Olympiacos

Premier League
Country: Israel
Founded: 1999
Most titles:
Maccabi Haifa - 7
2014 Champions:
Maccabi Tel Aviv

Tippeligaen
Country: Norway
Founded: 1937
Most titles: Rosenborg - 22
2013 Champions:
Stromsgodset IF

Ekstraklasa
Country: Poland
Founded: 1927
Most titles:
Legia Warsaw - 10
2014 Champions:
Legia Warsaw

Primeira Liga
Country: Portugal
Founded: 1934
Most titles: Benfica - 33
2014 Champions: Benfica

Liga 1
Country: Romania
Founded: 1909
Most titles:
Steaua Bucuresti - 25
2014 Champions:
Steaua Bucuresti

Premier League
Country: Russia
Founded: 2001
Most titles:
CSKA Moscow - 5
2014 Champions:
CSKA Moscow

SuperLiga
Country: Serbia
Founded: 2006
Most titles: FK Partizan - 6
2014 Champions:
Red Star

Corgon Liga
Country: Slovakia
Founded: 1993
Most titles:
SK Slovan Bratislava - 8
2014 Champions:
SK Slovan Bratislava

Allsvenskan
Country: Sweden
Founded: 1924
Most titles: Malmo FF - 20
2013 Champions:
Malmo FF

Super League
Country: Switzerland
Founded: 1897
Most titles:
Grasshopper - 27
2014 Champions: FC Basel

Super Lig
Country: Turkey
Founded: 1959
Most titles: Fenerbache,
Galatasaray - 19
2014 Champions:
Fenerbache

Premier League
Country: Ukraine
Founded: 1991
Most titles:
Dynamo Kiev - 13
2014 Champions:
Shakhtar Donetsk

Rest of the World

Winners from selected domestic leagues around the globe.

North America

MLS
Country: United States
Established: 1993
2013 champions: Sporting Kansas City
2013 top scorer: Camilo
(Vancouver Whitecaps) - 22
Most titles: D.C. United, LA Galaxy - 4

2012

South America

Campeonato Brasileiro Serie A
Country: Brazil
Established: 1959
2013 champions: Cruzeiro
2013 top scorer: Ederson
(Atletico Paranaense) - 21
Most titles: Santos, Palmeiras - 8

2009

Canadian Soccer League
Country: Canada
Established: 1926
2013 champions: SC Waterloo Region
2013 top scorer: Guillaume Surot
(Kingston FC) - 28
Most titles: Toronto Croatia - 9

Liga MX
Country: Mexico
Established: 1943
2014 champions: Club Leon
2014 top scorer: Pablo Velazquez (Toluca) -12
Most titles: America, Guadalajara - 11

Primera Division
Country: Argentina
Established: 1891
2014 champions: San Lorenzo
2014 top scorer: Mauro Zarate
(Vélez Sársfield) - 18
Most titles: River Plate - 36

Primera Division
Country: Uruguay
Established: 1900
2014 Champions: Danubio
2014 top scorer: Héctor Acuña (Cerro) - 20
Most titles: Penarol - 38

Asamoah Gyan (Al Ain)

Asia

J. League Division 1
Country: Japan
Established: 1992
2013 champions: Sanfrecce Hiroshima
2013 top scorer: Yoshito Okubo
(Kawasaki Frontale) -26
Most titles: Kashima Antlers - 7

K League
Country: South Korea
Established: 1983
2013 champions: Pohang Steelers
2013 top scorer: Dejan Damjanovic (FC Seoul),
Kim Shin-Wook (Ulsan Hyundai) - 19
Most titles: Seongnam FC - 7

UAE Arabian Gulf League
Country: United Arab Emirates
Established: 1973
2014 Champions: Al Ahli
2014 top scorer: Asamoah Gyan (Al Ain) - 29
Most titles: Al Ain - 11

Africa

Premier League
Country: Egypt
Established: 1948
**2011 (suspended in 2012 & 2013)
champions:** Al Ahly
2014 top scorer: Ahmed Abd El-Zaher (ENPPI),
Shikabala (Zamalek) - 13
Most titles: Al Ahly - 36

Premier Soccer League
Country: South Africa
Established: 1996
2014 Champions: Mamelodi Sundowns
2014 top scorer: Bernard Parker
(Kaiser Chiefs) -10
Most titles: Mamelodi Sundowns - 6

Ghana Premier League
Country: Ghana
Established: 1956
2014 champions: Asante Kotoko
2014 top scorer: Augustine Okrah (Bechem
United) - 16
Most titles: Asante Kotoko -24

Oceania

A-League
Country: Australia
Established: 2004
2014 champions: Brisbane Roar
2014 top scorer: Daniel McBreen
(Central Coast Mariners) - 17
Most titles: Central Coast Mariners,
Melbourne Victory, Brisbane Roar - 2

ASB Premiership
Country: New Zealand
Established: 2004
2014 champions: Auckland City FC
2014 top scorer: Emiliano Tade
(Auckland City FC) - 12
Most titles: Auckland City FC,
Waitakere United - 5

Club World Cup

T he Club World Cup first took place in Brazil in 2000. It's a seven team competition that consists of the champions from six continents (North America, South America, Asia, Africa, Europe and Oceania) along with the host nation's champions.

2012

Most wins: Barcelona, Corinthians - 2

Roll of Honour

2000 (Brazil) - Corinthians
2005 (Japan) - Sao Paulo
2006 (Japan) - Internacional
2007 (Japan) - AC Milan
2008 (Japan) - Manchester United
2009 (UAE) - Barcelona
2010 (UAE) - Internazionale
2011 (Japan) - Barcelona
2012 (Japan) - Corinthians
2013 (Morocco) - Bayern Munich

European Super Cup

T he European Super Cup is a match between the winners of the Champions League and the Europa League. The contest, first held in 1972, takes place at the start of each season.

1989

Most wins: AC Milan - 5

1993	Parma
1994	AC Milan
1995	Ajax
1996	Juventus
1997	Barcelona
1998	Chelsea
1999	Lazio
2000	Galatasaray
2001	Liverpool
2002	Real Madrid
2003	AC Milan
2004	Valencia
2005	Liverpool
2006	Sevilla
2007	AC Milan
2008	Zenit St. Petersburg
2009	Barcelona
2010	Atletico Madrid
2011	Barcelona
2012	Atletico Madrid
2013	Bayern Munich

Roll of Honour

1972	Ajax	**1982**	Aston Villa
1973	Ajax	**1983**	Aberdeen
1975	Dynamo Kiev	**1984**	Juventus
1976	Anderlecht	**1986**	Steaua Bucuresti
1977	Liverpool	**1987**	Porto
1978	Anderlecht	**1988**	Mechelen
1979	Nottingham Forest	**1989**	AC Milan
1980	Valencia	**1990**	AC Milan
		1991	Manchester United
		1992	Barcelona

International Competitions

nternational football has been around since England took on Scotland in the first official match between two countries in 1872. Despite regional competitions such as the British Home Nations Championship being played on an annual basis, the first true international tournament was held at the 1908 London Summer Olympic Games. The success of these tournaments, where all the players were amateurs, led to the creation of the FIFA World Cup in 1930. The competition is the biggest in the sport and has created the most magical and iconic moments the beautiful game has ever seen. Each continental governing body also have their own championship, which is a country's second biggest competition following the World Cup. The winners of each of these automatically qualify for the FIFA Confederations Cup, which takes place a year before each World Cup.

WORLD CUP

The FIFA World Cup is the pinnacle of the game and the biggest single-sporting event on the planet. Due to the success of international competition at the Olympic Games, FIFA president Jules Rimet, who the trophy was named after from 1930-1970, wanted to take that to a new level, leading to his proposal to stage the first ever World Cup two years later. His plan was put into action, leading to the inaugural tournament in Uruguay, which saw the hosts defeat Argentina in the final. The first edition of this great competition involved just 13 nations, with some countries refusing to recognise it as a major event, while others didn't have the resources to take part. This increased to 16, 24 and now to the current pool of 32 nations when the tournament expanded prior to the 1998 World Cup in France. The tournament will be held for the 20th time in Brazil this summer, who will be looking to add to their record five wins. The South American country is one of 16 nations (Korea Republic and Japan were joint hosts in 2002) to have hosted the competition which is held every four years and in its current format sees 207 teams enter the qualifying stage.

LAST TIME
(SOUTH AFRICA)

Winners: Spain **Runners-up:** Holland
Golden Boot: Thomas Muller (Germany) - 5 goals, 3 assists
Most assists: Dirk Kuyt (Holland), Kaka (Brazil), Bastian Schweinsteiger (Germany), Mesut Ozil (Germany), Thomas Muller (Germany) - 3
Player of the Tournament: Diego Forlan (Uruguay)
Most goals (team): Germany - 16 **Most goals against:** North Korea - 12 **Most clean sheets (team):** Spain - 5
Most clean sheets (player): Iker Casillas (Spain) -5
Biggest win: Portugal 7-0 North Korea
Highest scoring game: Portugal 7-0 North Korea
Biggest attendance: South Africa 1-1 Mexico, Holland 0-1 Spain - 84, 490 **Most yellow cards:** Holland - 23
Most red cards: Australia, Algeria, Brazil, Uruguay - 2

WORLD CUP GOLDEN BOOT (TOP SCORER)

1930	Guillermo Stabile (Argentina) - 8
1934	Oldrich Nejedly (Czechoslovakia) - 5
1938	Leonidas da Silva (Brazil) - 7
1950	Ademir (Brazil) - 8
1954	Sandor Kocsis (Hungary) - 11
1958	Just Fontaine (France) - 13
1962	Florian Albert (Hungary), Valentin Ivanov (Soviet Union), Garrincha, Vava (both Brazil), Drazen Jerkovic (Yugoslavia), Leonel Sanchez (Chile) - 4
1966	Eusebio (Portugal) - 9
1970	Gerd Muller (West Germany) - 10
1974	Grzegorz Lato (Poland) - 7
1978	Mario Kempes (Argentina) - 6
1982	Paolo Rossi (Italy) - 6
1986	Gary Lineker (England) - 6
1990	Salvatore Schillaci (Italy) - 6
1994	Oleg Salenko (Russia), Hristo Stoichkov (Bulgaria) - 4
1998	Davor Suker (Croatia) - 6
2002	Ronaldo (Brazil) - 8
2006	Miroslav Klose (Germany) - 5
2010	Thomas Muller (Germany) - 5

WORLD CUP GOLDEN BALL (BEST PLAYER)

1930	Jose Nasazzi (Uruguay)
1934	Giuseppe Meazza (Italy)
1938	Leonidas da Silva (Brazil)
1950	Zizinho (Brazil)
1954	Ferenc Puskas (Hungary)
1958	Didi (Brazil)
1962	Garrincha (Brazil)
1966	Bobby Charlton (England)
1970	Pele (Brazil)
1974	Johan Cruyff (Holland)
1978	Mario Kempes (Argentina)
1982	Paolo Rossi (Italy)
1986	Diego Maradona (Argentina)
1990	Salvatore Schillaci (Italy)
1994	Romario (Brazil)
1998	Ronaldo (Brazil)
2002	Oliver Khan (Germany)
2006	Zinedine Zidane (France)
2010	Diego Forlan (Uruguay)

ROLL OF HONOUR

1930 Uruguay
URUGUAY

1934 Italy
ITALY

1938 France
ITALY

1950 Brazil
URUGUAY

1954 Switzerland
WEST GERMANY

1958 Sweden
BRAZIL

1962 Chile
BRAZIL

1966 England
ENGLAND

1970 Mexico
BRAZIL

1974 West Germany
WEST GERMANY

1978 Argentina
ARGENTINA

1982 Spain
ITALY

1986 Mexico
ARGENTINA

1990 Italy
WEST GERMANY

1994 United States
BRAZIL

1998 France
FRANCE

2002 South Korea & Japan
BRAZIL

2006 Germany
ITALY

2010 South Africa
SPAIN

ALL TIME STATS

Most wins: Brazil - 5
Most final appearances: Brazil, Germany - 7
Most tournament appearances: Brazil - 20
Most final defeats: Germany - 4
Most winners' medals: Pele (Brazil) - 3
Top scorer: Ronaldo (Brazil) - 15
Most goals in a tournament:
Justin Fontaine (France) - 13 (1958)
Most appearances: Lothar Matthaus (Germany) - 25
Most tournaments: Antonio Carbajal (Mexico),
Lothar Matthaus (Germany) - 5
Most clean sheets: Iker Casillas (Spain),
Edwin van der Sar (Holland) - 9
Most goals: Brazil - 210
Most goals conceded: Germany - 117
Biggest crowd: Uruguay 2-1 Brazil -
171,772 (1950 Final)
Biggest win: Hungary 9-0 South Korea (1954),
Yugoslavia 9-0 Zaire (1974),
Hungary 10-1 El Salvador (1982)
Most goals in a game:
Austria 7-5 Switzerland (1954)
Oldest player: Roger Milla (Cameroon)
- 42 years, 39 days
Youngest player:
Norman Whiteside (Northern Ireland) -
17 years, 41 days

* All stats prior to 2014 World Cup

WORLD CUP GOLDEN GLOVE (BEST GOALKEEPER)

1930	Enrique Ballesteros (Uruguay)
1934	Ricardo Zamora (Spain)
1938	Frantisek Planicka (Czechoslovakia)
1950	Roque Maspoli (Uruguay)
1954	Gyula Grosics (Hungary)
1958	Harry Gregg (Northern Ireland)
1962	Villiam Schrojf (Czechoslovakia)
1966	Gordon Banks (England)
1970	Ladislao Mazurkiewicz (Uruguay)
1974	Sepp Maier (West Germany)
1978	Ubaldo Fillol (Argentina)
1982	Dino Zoff (Italy)
1986	Jean-Marie Pfaff (Belgium)
1990	Sergio Goycochea (Argentina)
1994	Michel Preud'homme (Belgium)
1998	Fabien Barthez (France)
2002	Oliver Khan (Germany)
2006	Gianluigi Buffon (Italy)
2010	Iker Casillas (Spain)

EUROPEAN CHAMPIONSHIP

The UEFA European Championship is the continent's major international football tournament. Held every four years since it first began in 1960, the competition has been won by nine different countries who have cemented their place in history. The first edition was hosted by France and consisted of just four teams. Soviet Union lifted the trophy after defeating Yugoslavia 2-1 in the final. The tournament was played out in this format until 1980, when it expanded to eight countries participating for the honour. This again changed in 1996, as another eight nations were thrown into the mix to take the total up to 16. The 2016 contest, in France, will see 53 teams enter the qualification stage and 24 play at the finals for the first time. Throughout the history of the event there has been one or two host countries, who have to win a bidding process in order to stage the tournament. However, Europe's governing body have again implemented a change which will see all Championships from Euro 2020 held in 13 cities across 13 different countries. Germany and Spain have both been crowned European Champions a record three times, and the Spaniards became the only team to win back-to-back titles when they beat Italy 4-0 in the 2012 final.

LAST TIME
(POLAND & UKRAINE)

Winners: Spain
Runners-up: Italy
Golden Boot: Fernando Torres (Spain) - 3 goals, 1 assist
Most assists: Steven Gerrard (England), Mesut Ozil (Germany), Andrei Arshavin (Russia), David Silva (Spain) - 3
Player of the Tournament: Andres Iniesta (Spain)
Most goals (team): Spain - 12
Most goals against: Republic of Ireland - 9
Most clean sheets (team): Spain - 5
Most clean sheets (player): Iker Casillas (Spain) - 5
Biggest win: Spain 4-0 Republic of Ireland, Spain 4-0 Italy
Highest scoring game: Germany 4-2 Greece
Biggest attendance: Sweden 2-3 England - 64, 640
Most yellow cards: Italy - 16
Most red cards: Greece, Republic of Ireland, Poland - 1

ROLL OF HONOUR

1960 France
SOVIET UNION

1964 Spain
SPAIN

1968 Italy
ITALY

1972 Belgium
WEST GERMANY

1976 Yugoslavia
CZECHOSLOVAKIA

1980 Italy
WEST GERMANY

1984 France
FRANCE

1988 West Germany
HOLLAND

1992 Sweden
DENMARK

1996 England
GERMANY

2000 Holland & Belgium
FRANCE

2004 Portugal
GREECE

2008 Austria & Switzerland
SPAIN

2012 Poland & Ukraine
SPAIN

1984

ALL TIME STATS

Most wins: Spain, Germany - 3
Most final appearances: Germany - 6
Most tournament appearances: Germany - 11
Most final defeats: Germany, Soviet Union - 3
Most winners' medals - Rainer Bonhof (Germany), Xabi Alonso, Iker Casillas, Cesc Fabregas, Andres Iniesta, Sergio Ramos, David Silva, Xavi Hernandez, Raul Albiol, Fernando Torres, Alvaro Arbeloa, Santi Cazorla, Pepe Reina (all Spain) - 2
Top scorer: Michel Platini (France) - 9
Most goals in a tournament: Michel Platini (France) - 9 (1984)
Most appearances: Lilian Thuram (France),
Edwin van der Sar (Holland) - 16
Most clean sheets: Iker Casillas (Spain),
Edwin van der Sar (Holland) - 9
Most goals: Germany - 65
Most goals conceded: Germany - 45
Biggest crowd: Spain 2-1 Soviet Union - 79,115 (1964 Final)
Biggest win: Holland 6-0 Yugoslavia (2000)
Most goals in a game: Yugoslavia 5-4 France (2000)
Oldest player: Lothar Matthaus (Germany) - 39 years, 91 days
Youngest player: Jetro Willems (Holland) - 18 years, 71 days

CONFEDERATIONS
CUP

Held in the World Cup's host country a year prior to football's biggest tournament, the Confederations Cup is seen as a dress-rehearsal to the sport's biggest event. The competition was first introduced in 1997 when FIFA took over and rebranded the King Fahd Cup, hosted in Saudi Arabia in 1992 and 1995. It was held every two years until 2005, when world football's governing body decided to have it every four years. The hosts, World Cup holders and the six continental champions qualify for the competition. Brazil have lifted the trophy a record four times and are the only country to have taken part in all seven tournaments to date.

LAST TIME
(BRAZIL)
Winners: Brazil
Runners-up: Spain
Golden Boot: Fernando Torres (Spain) - 5 goals
Most assists: Walter Gargano (Uruguay) - 3
Player of the Tournament: Neymar (Brazil)
Most goals (team): Spain - 15
Most goals against: Tahiti - 24
Most clean sheets (team): Brazil, Spain - 3
Most clean sheets (player): Julio Cesar (Brazil), Iker Casillas (Spain) - 5
Biggest win: Spain 10-0 Tahiti
Highest scoring game: Spain 10-0 Tahiti
Biggest attendance: Brazil 3-0 Spain - 73,351
Most yellow cards: Uruguay - 10
Most red cards: Spain, Italy, Tahiti, Uruguay - 1

ALL-TIME STATS

Most wins: Brazil - 4
Most final appearances: Brazil - 5
Most tournament appearances: Brazil - 7
Most final defeats: Argentina - 2
Top scorer: Cuauhtemoc Blanco (Mexico), Ronaldinho (Brazil) - 9
Most goals in a tournament: Romario (Brazil) - 7 (1997)
Most appearances: Dida (Brazil) - 22
Most clean sheets: Dida (Brazil) - 9
Most goals: Brazil - 78
Most goals conceded: Mexico - 31
Biggest crowd: Mexico 4-3 Brazil - 110,000 (1999 Final)
Biggest win: Spain 10-0 Tahiti (2013)
Most goals in a game: Spain 10-0 Tahiti (2013), Brazil 8-2 Saudi Arabia (1999)
Oldest player: Ali Boumnijel (Tunisia) - 39 years, 67 days
Youngest player: Chris Wood (New Zealand) - 17 years, 193 days

COPA AMERICA

The Copa America was founded in 1916 and first known as the South American Championship. The tournament, which is the oldest international continental competition, is now contested ever four years to determine the champions of South America. Twelve teams compete, but because the South American Football Confederation consists of just ten members the likes of Costa Rica, USA and Mexico have recently been invited to fill the two extra spots.

ROLL OF HONOUR

South American Championship
1916 Argentina **URUGUAY**
1917 Uruguay **URUGUAY**
1919 Brazil **BRAZIL**
1920 Chile **URUGUAY**
1921 Argentina **ARGENTINA**
1922 Brazil **BRAZIL**
1923 Uruguay **URUGUAY**
1924 Uruguay **URUGUAY**
1925 Argentina **ARGENTINA**
1926 Chile **URUGUAY**
1927 Peru **ARGENTINA**
1929 Argentina **ARGENTINA**
1935 Peru **URUGUAY**
1937 Argentina **ARGENTINA**
1939 Peru **PERU**
1941 Chile **ARGENTINA**
1942 Uruguay **URUGUAY**
1945 Chile **ARGENTINA**
1946 Argentina **ARGENTINA**
1947 Ecuador **ARGENTINA**
1949 Brazil **BRAZIL**
1953 Peru **PARAGUAY**

1955 Chile **ARGENTINA**
1956 Uruguay **URUGUAY**
1957 Peru **ARGENTINA**
1959 Argentina **ARGENTINA**
1959 Ecuador **URUGUAY**
1963 Bolivia **BOLIVIA**
1967 Uruguay **URUGUAY**

Copa America
1975 no one host **PERU**
1979 no one host **PARAGUAY**
1983 no one host **URUGUAY**
1987 Argentina **URUGUAY**
1989 Brazil **BRAZIL**
1991 Chile **ARGENTINA**
1993 Ecuador **ARGENTINA**
1995 Uruguay **URUGUAY**
1997 Bolivia **BRAZIL**
1999 Paraguay **BRAZIL**
2001 Colombia **COLOMBIA**
2004 Peru **BRAZIL**
2007 Venezuela **BRAZIL**
2011 Argentina **URUGUAY**

LAST TIME
(ARGENTINA)

Winners: Uruguay
Runners-up: Paraguay
Top scorer: Paolo Guerrero (Peru) - 5
Player of the Tournament:
Luis Suarez (Uruguay)
Biggest attendance:
Uruguay 3-0 Paraguay - 57, 921

ALL-TIME STATS

Most wins: Uruguay - 15
Most final appearances: Argentina - 26
Most tournament appearances: Uruguay - 40
Most final defeats: Argentina - 12
Top scorer: Norberto Mendez (Argentina),
Zizinho (Brazil) - 17
Most appearances:
Sergio Livingstone (Chile) - 34

AFRICA CUP OF NATIONS

A frica's biggest football tournament has been running since 1957 and is now held every two years in January - except when it was moved to odd-numbered years from 2013, preventing it from clashing with the World Cup. Three teams took part in the first edition which was hosted by Sudan and won by Egypt, who are the competition's most successful country having lifted the trophy seven times. This tournament's format has been expanded by the Confederation of African Football throughout its history, leading to 16 participating nations since 1998, held in Burkina Faso.

LAST TIME
(SOUTH AFRICA)

Winners: Nigeria
Runners-up: Burkina Faso
Top scorer: Emmanuel Emenike (Nigeria),
Wakaso Mubarek (Ghana) - 4
Player of the Tournament:
Jonathan Pitroipa (Burkina Faso)
Biggest attendance:
Nigeria 1-0 Burkina Faso - 85,000

ROLL OF HONOUR

1957 Sudan **EGYPT**
1959 Egypt **EGYPT**
1962 Ethiopia **ETHIOPIA**
1963 Ghana **GHANA**
1965 Tunisia **GHANA**
1968 Ethiopia **CONGO DR**
1970 Sundan **SUDAN**
1972 Cameroon **CONGO**
1974 Egypt **ZAIRE**
1976 Ethiopia **MOROCCO**
1978 Ghana **GHANA**
1980 Nigeria **NIGERIA**
1982 Libya **GHANA**
1984 Ivory Coast **CAMEROON**
1986 Egypt **EGYPT**
1988 Morocco **CAMEROON**
1990 Algeria **ALGERIA**
1992 Senegal **IVORY COAST**
1994 Tunisia **NIGERIA**
1996 South Africa **SOUTH AFRICA**
1998 Burkina Faso **EGPYT**
2000 Ghana/Nigeria **CAMEROON**
2002 Mali **CAMEROON**
2004 Tunisia **TUNISIA**
2006 Egypt **EGYPT**
2008 Ghana **EGYPT**
2010 Angola **EGYPT**
2012 Gabon/Equatorial Guinea **ZAMBIA**
2013 South Africa **NIGERIA**

ALL-TIME STATS

Most wins: Egypt - 7
Most final appearances: Egypt, Ghana - 8
Most tournament appearances:
Egypt - 22
Most final defeats: Ghana, Nigeria - 4
Top scorer: Samuel Eto'o (Cameroon) - 18
Most appearances: Rigobert Song
(Cameroon) - 33

OTHER CONTINENTS

As well as Europe, South America and Africa, major continental competitions are held in North America, Oceania and Asia.

CONCACAF GOLD CUP

Continent: North America
Founded: 1991
Most wins: Mexico - 6
Most final appearances: United States - 9
Most tournament appearances: Mexico, United States - 12
Most final defeats: United States - 4
Top scorer: Landon Donovan (United States) - 18

LAST TIME (UNITED STATES)

Winners: United States
Runners-up: Panama
Top scorer: Gabriel Torres (Panama), Landon Donovan, Chris Wondolowski (both United States) - 5
Player of the Tournament: Landon Donovan (United States)
Biggest attendance: United States 3-1 Honduras - 81,410

OFC NATIONS CUP

Continent: Oceania
Founded: 1973
Most wins: Australia, New Zealand - 4
Most final appearances: Australia - 6
Most tournament appearances: New Zealand - 9
Most final defeats: Tahiti - 3
Top scorer: Damian Mori (Australia) - 14

LAST TIME (SOLOMON ISLANDS)

Winners: Tahiti
Runners-up: New Caledonia
Top scorer: Jacques Haeko (New Caledonia) - 6
Player of the Tournament: Nicolas Vallar (Tahiti)
Biggest attendance: New Zealand 1-1 Solomon Islands - 18,000

AFC ASIAN CUP

Continent: Asia
Founded: 1956
Most wins: Japan - 4
Most final appearances: Saudi Arabia - 6
Most tournament appearances: Iran, South Korea - 13
Most final defeats: Saudi Arabia, South Korea - 3
Top scorer: Ali Daei (Iran) - 14

LAST TIME (QATAR)

Winners: Japan
Runners-up: Australia (moved from OFC Nations Cup in 2007)
Top scorer: Koo Ja-Cheol (South Korea) - 5
Player of the Tournament: Keisuke Honda (Japan)
Biggest attendance: Australia 0-1 Japan (a.e.t.) - 37,174

Landon Donovan

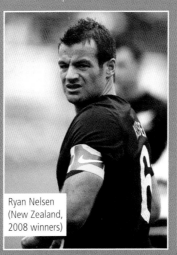
Ryan Nelsen (New Zealand, 2008 winners)

Ali Daei

FIFA Ballon d'Or

The FIFA Ballon d'Or is the most prestigious accolade any player can receive in world football. It is recognition of a player's place among the greats and testament to the level of their performances throughout the previous year.

The award has been in existence since 1956 but right up until 1995 only players from Europe were considered, meaning legends such as Pele and Diego Maradona never received it. Even with the changes in 1995, the nominated players still had to play in Europe to be in contention which remained the case until the award finally became global in 2007.

In 2010 it merged with the FIFA World Player of the Year Award and was therefore renamed the FIFA Ballon d'Or.

We take a look at the great players to have collected the gold ball.

PAST WINNERS

1956 - Stanley Matthews	1974 - Johan Cruyff	1994 - Hristo Stoichkov
1957 - Alfredo Di Stefano	1975 - Oleg Blokhin	1995 - George Weah
1958 - Raymond Kopa	1976 - Franz Beckenbauer	1996 - Matthias Sammer
1959 - Alfredo Di Stefano	1977 - Allan Simonsen	1997 - Ronaldo
1960 - Luis Suarez	1978 - Kevin Keegan	1998 - Zinedine Zidane
1961 - Omar Sivori	1979 - Kevin Keegan	1999 - Rivaldo
1962 - Josef Masopust	1980 - Karl-Heinz Rummenigge	2000 - Luis Figo
1963 - Lev Yashin	1981 - Karl-Heinz Rummenigge	2001 - Michael Owen
1964 - Denis Law	1982 - Paolo Rossi	2002 - Ronaldo
1965 - Eusebio	1983 - Michel Platini	2003 - Pavel Nedved
1966 - Bobby Charlton	1984 - Michel Platini	2004 - Andrei Shevchenko
1967 - Florian Albert	1985 - Michel Platini	2005 - Ronaldinho
1968 - George Best	1986 - Igor Belanov	2006 - Fabio Cannavaro
1969 - Gianni Rivera	1987 - Ruud Gullit	2007 - Kaka
1970 - Gerd Muller	1988 - Marco van Basten	2008 - Cristiano Ronaldo
1971 - Johan Cruyff	1989 - Marco van Basten	2009 - Lionel Messi
1972 - Franz Beckenbauer	1990 - Lothar Matthaus	2010 - Lionel Messi
1973 - Johan Cruyff	1991 - Jean-Pierre Papin	2011 - Lionel Messi
	1992 - Marco van Basten	2012 - Lionel Messi
	1993 - Roberto Baggio	2013 - Cristiano Ronaldo

WINNERS BY CLUB

1st

Barcelona
Winners - 10: Lionel Messi (4), Johan Cruyff (2), Ronaldinho, Rivaldo, Hristo Stoichkov, Luis Suarez

2nd

Juventus
Winners - 8: Michel Platini (3), Pavel Nedved, Zinedine Zidane, Roberto Baggio, Paolo Rossi, Omar Sivori,

Milan
Winners - 8: Marco van Basten (3), Ruud Gullit, Kaka, Andriy Shevchenko, George Weah, Gianni Rivera

4th

Real Madrid
Winners - 7: Alfredo di Stefano (2), Cristiano Ronaldo, Fabio Cannavaro, Ronaldo, Luis Figo, Raymond Kopa,

5th

Bayern Munich
Winners - 5: Karl Heinz Rummenigge (2), Franz Beckenbauer (2), Gerd Muller

6th

Manchester United
Winners - 4: Cristiano Ronaldo, George Best, Bobby Charlton, Denis Law

BY NATIONALITY

1st

Germany
Winners - 7: Karl-Heinz Rummenigge (2), Franz Beckenbauer (2), Matthias Sammer, Lothar Matthaus, Gerd Muller

Holland
Winners - 7: Marco van Basten (3), Johan Cruyff (3), Ruud Gullit

3rd

Argentina
Winners - 6: Lionel Messi (4), Alfredo di Stefano (won second representing Spain), Omar Sivori

France
Winners - 6: Michel Platini (3), Zinedine Zidane, Jean-Pierre Papin, Raymond Kopa,

5th

Brazil
Winners - 5: Ronaldo (2), Kaka, Ronaldinho, Rivaldo

England
Winners - 5: Kevin Keegan (2), Michael Owen, Bobby Charlton, Stanley Matthews

7th

Italy
Winners - 4: Fabio Cannavaro, Roberto Baggio, Palo Rossi, Gianni Rivera

Portugal
Winners - 4: Cristiano Ronaldo (2), Luis Figo, Eusebio

CRISTIANO RONALDO

Position: Forward
Birth date: February 5, 1985
Birth place: Madeira, Portugal
Height: 1.85m (6ft 1in)
Clubs: Sporting CP, Manchester United, Real Madrid
International: Portugal
Ballon d'Or wins: 2 (2008, 2013)

Cristiano Ronaldo is the latest recipient of the Ballon d'Or having collected it in January 2014. He was first recognised as the world's best player in 2008 after scoring 42 times in 49 games for Manchester United. A then world-record £80m transfer to Real Madrid happened just over a year later and the explosive forward has gone from strength to strength in Spain, scoring more than a goal per game over the past five seasons. He's won four honours at the Bernabeu and is captain for both his club and the Portugal national team.

LIONEL MESSI

Position: Forward
Birth date: June 24, 1987
Birth place: Rosario, Argentina
Height: 1.69m (5ft 7in)
Clubs: Barcelona
International: Argentina
Ballon d'Or wins: 4
(2009, 2010, 2011, 2012)

To many, Lionel Messi is seen as the greatest player ever. The Argentina star joined Barcelona at the age of 12 and 15 years later has broken nearly every record there is to break. The attacker has won 21 honours with the Catalan side, is the club's all-time record scorer and has been crowned the world's best player a record four times. The South American magician also recorded the most goals in a calendar year when he scored 91 in 2012, captains his country and holds countless individual records that may never be bettered.

FIFA
Ballon d'Or
Previous Winners

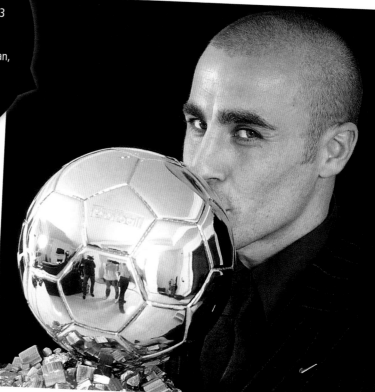

KAKA
Position: Midfielder
Birth date: April 22, 1982
Birth place: Gama, Brazil
Height: 1.86m (6ft 1in)
Clubs: Sao Paulo, AC Milan, Real Madrid
International: Brazil
Ballon d'Or wins: 1 (2007)

Kaka is often regarded as one of Brazil's most talented stars, and it's easy to see why. His most successful spell was at AC Milan, where he won the Serie A title in 2004 and the Champions League in 2007. It was in this magical year that saw him win the Ballon d'Or. He was part of the Brazil side that won their fifth World Cup in 2002, and moved from Milan to Real Madrid for a whopping £56m in 2009. He failed to flourish in Spain and returned to Milan in 2013.

FABIO CANNAVARO
Position: Defender
Birth date: September 13, 1973
Birth place: Naples, Italy
Height: 1.76m (5ft 9in)
Clubs: Napoli, Parma, Inter Milan, Juventus, Real Madrid, Al-Ahli
International: Italy
Ballon d'Or wins: 1 (2006)

Known as The Berlin Wall by his Italian fans, Cannavaro is widely regarded as one of the greatest defenders of all time. Having spent most of his career in his home country, he won two Coppa Italias with Parma as well as the UEFA Cup in 1999. He has also lifted two league titles in Spain with Real Madrid, but the highlight of his career came in 2006 when he captained Italy to World Cup glory. It was that year he won the Ballon d'Or and was named Serie A footballer of the year.

RONALDINHO

Position: Forward
Birth date: March 21, 1980
Birth place: Porto Alegre, Brazil
Height: 1.81m (5ft 11in)
Clubs: Gremio, Paris Saint-Germain, Barcelona, AC Milan, Flamengo, Atletico Mineiro
International: Brazil
Ballon d'Or wins: 1 (2005)

FIFA
Ballon d'Or
Previous
Winners

Renowned for his tricky footwork and his technique, Ronaldinho is one of the most exciting players to have graced a football pitch. It was at Barcelona, after rejecting Manchester United, where he became one of the greats. The Porto Alegre-born star would go on to win the Champions League and two La Liga titles with Barca, scoring 70 goals in 145 games. He was also instrumental in winning the World Cup with Brazil in 2002 where he famously scored a free-kick against England.

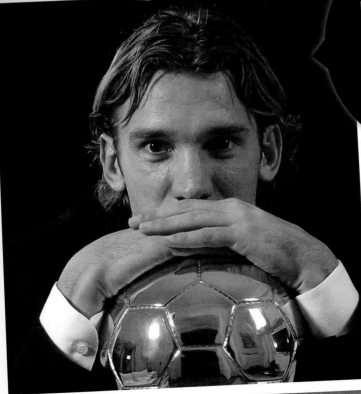

ANDRIY SHEVCHENKO

Position: Striker
Birth date: September 29, 1976
Birth place: Dvirkivschyna, Ukrainian SSR, Soviet Union
Height: 1.83m (6ft 0in)
Clubs: Dyamo Kyiv, AC Milan, Chelsea, AC Milan (on loan), Dynamo Kyiv
International: Ukraine
Ballon d'Or wins: 1(2004)

Andriy Shevchenko's CV is nothing short of impressive having won the Champions League, Serie A, FA Cup and five Ukrainian Premier Leagues. It was at Milan where he enjoyed his most successful spell, finishing top scorer in Italy in his debut season. He scored the winning penalty in the 2003 Champions League final, becoming the first Ukrainian to win the trophy. He is also Ukraine's all-time top scorer with 48 goals in 111 games.

FIFA

Ballon d'Or
Previous
Winners

Pavel Nedved is one of the most technically gifted players to have come out of Europe. He is arguably the greatest Czechoslovakian player of all time and only the second man from his country to have won the Ballon d'Or. He rose to prominence in 1996 when the Czech Republic reached the European Championship final. Since then he moved to Italy to play for Lazio and Juventus, but it was at the latter where he earned himself the prestigious award, playing 247 times after securing a £25m transfer in 2001.

Having had a successful spell at PSV, Ronaldo moved to Barcelona in 1996. He would go on to score 47 goals in 49 games for them that campaign to win his first Ballon d'Or. The highlight of his illustrious career came in 2002 when Brazil won the World Cup and clinched the Golden Boot. He then went on to win three trophies with Real Madrid after a £28.5m move. R9 scored 62 goals in 98 matches for Brazil and is currently the highest goalscorer in World Cup finals history with 15 goals.

MICHAEL OWEN

Position: Striker
Birth date: December 14, 1979
Birth place: Chester, England
Height: 1.73m (5ft 8in)
Clubs: Liverpool, Real Madrid, Newcastle United, Manchester United, Stoke City
International: England
Ballon d'Or wins: 1 (2001)

Michael Owen made his name at Liverpool, where he came through the club's academy. He scored on his debut against Wimbledon, and was the joint top scorer in the Premier League in the 1997-98 season. In 2001, Liverpool won a cup treble, and Owen collected the Ballon d'Or the same year. He left Liverpool for Real Madrid in 2004 for £8m, before returning to England for Newcastle. In 1998, aged 18, he scored a wonderful solo effort against Argentina at the World Cup before going on to score 40 times in 89 caps for his country.

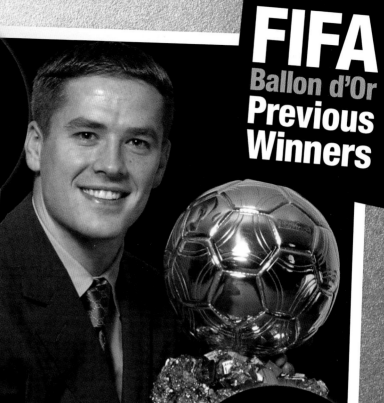

LUIS FIGO

Position: Midfielder
Birth date: November 4, 1972
Birth place: Lisbon, Portugal
Height: 1.80m (5ft 11in)
Clubs: Sporting Lisbon, Barcelona, Real Madrid, Inter Milan
International: Portugal
Ballon d'Or wins: 1 (2000)

Luis Figo was a midfield maestro and is one of Portugal's finest ever players. Having worked his way through Sporting Lisbon's youth system, the winger made his first senior appearance for the club in 1989. He won his first international cap for Portugal in 1991 and would go on to play a record 127 times for them. He is one of only a few players to play for both Barcelona and Real Madrid and has an impressive trophy cabinet, which includes four La Liga titles, four Serie A trophies and a Champions League winner's medal.

FIFA
Ballon d'Or
Previous
Winners

RIVALDO
Position: Midfielder
Birth date: April 19, 1972
Birth place: Paulista, Brazil
Height: 1.86m (6ft 1in)
Clubs: Santa Cruz, Mogi Mirim, Corinthians (on loan), Palmeiras, Deportivo La Coruna, Barcelona, AC Milan, Cruzeiro (on loan), Olympiacos AEK Athens, Bunyodkor, Sao Paulo (on loan), Kabuscorp, Sao Caetano
International: Brazil
Ballon d'Or wins: 1 (1999)

Rivaldo worked his way up from poverty to become one of the top midfielders on the planet. He is best known for his time at Barcelona, where he scored 19 goals in his first season with the club in 1999, winning the La Liga title and the Ballon d'Or award. He won 25 honours throughout his glittering career, including the Champions League, two La Liga crowns plus the 1999 Copa America and 2002 World Cup with Brazil.

ZINEDINE ZIDANE
Position: Midfielder
Birth date: June 23, 1972
Birth place: Marseille, France
Height: 1.85 (6ft 1in)
Clubs: Cannes, Bordeaux, Juventus, Real Madrid
International: France
Ballon d'Or wins: 1 (1998)

Despite his sending off for a headbutt in the 2006 World Cup final, Zidane will always be remembered as one of the greatest players ever. Zizou's trophy cabinet is incredible, he has won the World Cup and European Championship with France plus the Champions League and La Liga with Real Madrid and two Serie A titles with Juventus. The playmaker scored twice in the 1998 World Cup final against Brazil and a stunning volley in the 2003 Champions League final versus Bayer Leverkusen.

MATTHIAS SAMMER

Position: Midfielder
Birth date: September 5, 1967
Birth place: Dresden, Germany
Height: 1.8m (5 ft 11in)
Clubs: Dynamo Dresden, VFB Stuttgart, Inter Milan, Borussia Dortmund
International: East Germany, Germany
Ballon d'Or wins: 1 (1996)

Sammer had a luxurious career. He helped Borussia Dortmund to back-to-back league titles in the 1994-95 and 1995-96 seasons, and the DFB-Supercup in 1996, helping him win the Ballon d'Or. In 1997, he captained the club to their first ever Champions League title and Intercontinental Cup. He also won the European Championship with Germany in 1996 and was named player of the tournament.

GEORGE WEAH

Position: Striker
Birth date: October 1, 1966
Birth place: Monrovia, Liberia
Height: 1.84m (6ft ½ in)
Clubs: Mighty Barrolle, Invincible Eleven, Africa Sports, Tonnerre Yaoundé, Monaco, Paris Saint-Germain, AC Milan, Chelsea (on loan), Manchester City, Marseille, Al-Jazira
International: Liberia
Ballon d'Or wins: 1 (1995)

Monaco brought Weah to Europe in 1988 courtesy of then manager Arsene Wenger. The striker was to have a successful career on the continent as he won Ligue 1 with PSG in 1994 and was the top scorer in the Champions League in 1995 - the same year he became the first African player to win the Ballon d'Or. He then went on to play for AC Milan, Chelsea, Manchester City and Marseille in a career which produced 193 goals in 478 games.

FIFA
Ballon d'Or
Previous Winners

HRISTO STOICHKOV
Position: Forward
Birth date: February 8, 1966
Birth place: Plovdiv, Bulgaria
Height: 1.78m (5ft 10 in)
Clubs: Hebros, CSKA Sofia, Barcelona, Parma, Al-Nassr, Kashiwa Reysol, Chicago Fire, D.C. United
International: Bulgaria
Ballon d'Or wins: 1 (1994)

Stoichkov began his career in Bulgaria before signing for European giants Barcelona in 1990. He had a successful spell and was part of the 'Dream Team' at the Camp Nou, winning four La Liga titles and one Champions League. In 1994 Stoichkov led Bulgaria to fourth place in the World Cup, where he also won the Golden Boot by netting six times, leading to him collecting the Ballon d'Or. With an impressive 225 goals in 473 career matches, Stoichkov is seen as the greatest Bulgarian player of all time.

ROBERTO BAGGIO
Position: Forward
Birth date: February 18, 1967
Birth place: Caldogno, Italy
Height: 1.74m (5ft 8 ½)
Clubs: Vicenza, Fiorentina, Juventus, AC Milan, Bologna, Inter Milan, Brescia
International: Italy
Ballon d'Or wins: 1 (1993)

Famous for his ponytail, Roberto Baggio lit up Italian football in the 1990s. The playmaker has the record for being the only Italian to score in three World Cups, and is his country's fourth all-time top scorer with 27 goals in 56 caps. His Ballon d'Or win came after helping Juventus to UEFA Cup glory in 1993. Baggio missed the decisive penalty in the '94 World Cup final which handed victory to Brazil, but the man that played for Italian giants Internazionale, AC Milan and Juventus became the first Italian player in over 50 years to score 300 career goals in 2002.

MARCO VAN BASTEN

Position: Striker
Birth date: October 31, 1964
Birth place: Utrecht, Holland
Height: 1.88m (6ft 2in)
Clubs: Ajax, AC Milan
International: Holland
Ballon d'Or wins: 3 (1992, 1989, 1988)

Having scored 277 goals in his illustrious career, it is easy to see why Marco van Basten is regarded as one of the greatest strikers of all time. The Dutchman won three League titles at Ajax and AC Milan, and helped Holland to European Championship glory in 1988 where he finished as the competition's top scorer. His three Ballon d'Or wins in 1992, 1989 and 1988 added to an impressive list of honours before he was sadly forced to retire at the age of 28 with an ankle injury. Van Basten later took up management and had spells coaching Holland and Ajax.

JEAN-PIERRE PAPIN

Position: Striker
Birth date: November 5, 1963
Birth place: Boulogne-sur-Mer, France
Height: 1.76m (5ft 9 in)
Clubs: Valenciennes, Club Brugge, Marseille, AC Milan, Bayern Munich, Bordeaux, Guingamp, Saint-Pierroise
International: France
Ballon d'Or wins: 1 (1991)

Jean-Pierre Papin will be remembered for his stunning goals and trademark volleys. The Frenchman enjoyed a highly successful time at Marseille where he won four French League titles in a row between 1989-1992, collecting the Ballon d'Or in the process. He was also the league's topscorer for five consecutive seasons before AC Milan signed him for a world record £10m in 1992. Papin was also lethal at international level as he struck 30 times in 54 caps for France.

FIFA
Ballon d'Or
Previous
Winners

LOTHAR MATTHAUS
Position: Midfielder
Birth date: March 21, 1961
Birth place: Erlangen, West Germany
Height: 1.74m (5ft 9in)
Clubs: Borussia Monchengladbach, Bayern Munich, Internazionale, Bayern Munich, MetroStars
International: Germany
Ballon d'Or wins: 1 (1990)

Matthaus had an incredibly long career at the top of the game, playing 20 years for Germany. The midfielder is his country's record caps holder having represented them 150 times. He played in five World Cups and was captain as West Germany lifted the trophy in 1990. The super skipper also won the European Championship in 1980 and collected 23 honours in a club career that saw him represent Borussia Monchengladbach, Bayern Munich, Internazionale and MetroStars.

RUUD GULLIT
Position: Midfielder
Birth date: September 16, 1962
Birth place: Amsetrdam, Holland
Height: 1.91m (6ft 3in)
Clubs: HFC Harlem, Feyenoord, PSV, AC Milan, Sampdoria, Chelsea
International: Holland
Ballon d'Or wins: 1 (1987)

After impressing in his homeland, Gullit grabbed the attention of the world when he moved to AC Milan in 1987. At the San Siro the midfielder won three Serie A titles, two Italian Super Cups, two European Cups, two UEFA Super Cups and two Intercontinental Cups. The charismatic playmaker also helped his country win the 1988 European Championship in an international career which saw him earn 66 caps. The Amsterdam-born star took up a player-manager role at Chelsea in 1996 and he guided the Blues to the FA Cup a year later.

IGOR BELANOV

Position: Midfielder
Birth date: September 25, 1960
Birth place: Odessa, Ukraine SSR, Soviet Union
Height: 1.74m (5ft 9in)
Clubs: SKA Odessa, Chornomorets Odessa, Dynamo Kiev, Borussia Monchengladbach, Eintracht Braunschweig, Metalurh Mariupol
International: Soviet Union
Ballon d'Or wins: 1 (1986)

Belanov started out at his hometown club Odessa before going on to become one of the greatest midfielders in the 1980s. His move to Dynamo Kiev in 1985 catapulted him into the spotlight and a year later he was picking up the prestigious Ballon d'Or after helping the Ukrainian club to a league and cup double. Two years later he was a key part of the Soviet Union squad that lost to Holland in the Euro '88 final. Belanov scored eight times in 33 appearances for the country.

MICHEL PLATINI

Position: Midfielder
Birth date: June 21, 1955
Birth place: Joeuf, France
Height: 1.77m (5ft 10in)
Clubs: Nancy, Saint-Etienne, Juventus
International: France
Ballon d'Or wins: 3 (1985, 1984, 1983)

Platini was a midfield master and arguably Europe's greatest ever player. He scored 41 times in 72 appearances for France, captaining them to European Championship glory on their own patch in 1984. He also played at three World Cups and won 10 honours in his club career. The current president of UEFA is only one of four men to have won the Ballon d'Or three times, all of which he was awarded during his time at Juventus where he won back-to-back Serie A titles and the European Cup.

FIFA
Ballon d'Or
Previous
Winners

PAOLO ROSSI
Position: Striker
Birth date: September 23, 1956
Birth place: Prato, Itlay
Height: 1.78m (5ft 10in)
Clubs: Juventus, Como (loan), Vicenza, Perugia (loan), AC Milan, Hellas Verona
International: Italy
Ballon d'Or wins: 1 (1982)

After impressing at Vicenza, Rossi was snapped up by Juventus where he won six trophies in four seasons. Despite having played just three games in two years, due to a ban for match fixing, he was selected for the 1982 World Cup where he helped his country to their third victory. Rossi also collected the Golden Boot and Golden Ball to become only the second player to win all three honours at the tournament after Argentina's Mario Kempes did it in 1978.

KARL-HEINZ RUMMENIGGE
Position: Striker
Birth date: September 25, 1955
Birth place: Lippstadt, West Germany
Height: 1.82m (5ft 11in)
Clubs: Bayern Munich, Internazionale, Servette FC
International: Germany
Ballon d'Or wins: 2 (1981, 1980)

The German is just one of six players to have won back-to-back Ballon d'Or trophies. He spent 10 years in his homeland with Bayern Munich where he enjoyed the most successful time of his career, winning the European Cup, Intercontinental Cup, two Bundesliga titles and two German Cups. He was a key member of West Germany's 1980 European Championship winning side and was the second top scorer at the 1982 World Cup where his country finished runners-up to Italy.

FIFA
Ballon d'Or
Previous
Winners

KEVIN KEEGAN
Position: Forward
Birth date: February 14, 1951
Birth place: Doncaster, England
Height: 1.73m (5ft 8in)
Clubs: Scunthorpe United, Liverpool, Hamburg SV, Southampton, Newcastle United, Blacktown City
International: England
Ballon d'Or wins: 2 (1979, 1978)

Despite spending the majority of his career in England, Keegan was twice recognised as the world's best player in his three-year spell with German side Hamburg. His 40 goals in 111 games helped the side to one Bundesliga title and a European Cup final before a surprise £500,000 move to Southampton in 1980. Keegan also collected nine honours with Liverpool and scored 21 times in 63 matches for England. The forward had spells managing Newcastle United, Fulham, England and Manchester City after hanging up his boots.

ALLAN SIMONSEN
Position: Striker
Birth date: December 15, 1952
Birth place: Vejle, Denmark
Height: 1.65m (5ft 5in)
Clubs: Velje BK, Borussia Monchengladbach, Barcelona, Charlton Athletic
International: Denmark
Ballon d'Or wins: 1 (1977)

An often forgotten winner but one of Denmark's greatest ever players. Simonsen's impressive haul of 76 goals in 176 matches, which helped Monchengladbach to three consecutive Bundesliga titles and two UEFA Cups in the 70s, saw him collect the Ballon d'Or in 1977. The Dane's form caught the attention of Barcelona where he won the Spanish Cup and European Cup Winners' Cup. The attacker also had a brief spell in England after making a shock move from the Camp Nou to Charlton Athletic in 1982.

FIFA
Ballon d'Or
Previous Winners

FRANZ BECKENBAUER

Position: Defender/Midfielder
Birth date: September 11, 1945
Birth place: Munich, Germany
Height: 1.81m (5ft 11in)
Clubs: Bayern Munich, New York Cosmos, Hamburg SV
International: Germany
Ballon d'Or wins: 2 (1976, 1972)

Der Kaiser is not just one of the greatest captains the world has ever seen, but one of the greatest players too. A leader through his showings at the back for club and country, the sweeper lifted 13 trophies including four league titles and three European Cups in his 13 years at Bayern Munich. He also skippered Germany to the 1974 World Cup and 1972 European Championship trophy. After retiring, Beckenbauer managed Germany to the 1990 World Cup.

OLEG BLOKHIN

Position: Forward
Birth date: November 5, 1952
Birth place: Kiev, Ukrainian SSR, Soviet Union
Height: 1.80m (5ft 11in)
Clubs: Dynamo Kiev, Vorwarts Steyr, Aris Limassol
International: Soviet Union
Ballon d'Or wins: 1 (1975)

One of Eastern Europe's greatest ever players was deadly in the final third. Nineteen of his 21-year career was spent at hometown club Dynamo Kiev where he is the club's record goalscorer with 266 goals. Blokhin is also the top scorer for the now disassembled Soviet Union national team and in the history of the Soviet Top League. He won 19 honours with the Kiev club and represented the national team at two World Cups. Since retiring, he has managed a whole host of clubs across Europe and is currently the head coach at his former club, Dynamo Kiev.

JOHAN CRUYFF

Position: Forward
Birth date: April 25, 1947
Birth place: Amsterdam, Holland
Height: 1.80m (5ft 11in)
Clubs: Ajax, Barcelona, LA Aztecs, Washington Diplomats, Levante, Ajax, Feyenoord
International: Holland
Ballon d'Or wins: 3 (1974, 1973, 1971)

The man who invented the Cruyff turn is just one of four players to have won the award three times and just one of four to win it at two different clubs (Ajax and Barcelona). The Dutch master won 20 honours at the Amsterdam club including eight Eredivisie titles and three European Cups. His move to Barcelona brought 63 goals in 184 games plus the 1974 La Liga championship and 1978 Spanish Cup. The superstar scored 33 times in 48 caps for Holland and is often regarded as the best player never to have won the World Cup.

GERD MULLER

Position: Striker
Birth date: November 3, 1945
Birth place: Nordlingen, Germany
Height: 1.76m (5ft 10in)
Clubs: 1861 Nordlingen, Bayern Munich, Fort Lauderdale Strikers
International: Germany
Ballon d'Or wins: 1 (1970)

Third top scorer at the World Cup finals, Muller scored for fun throughout his career. At Bayern Munich, The Bomber won three European Cups, four Bundesliga titles, the European Cup Winners' Cup, Intercontinental Cup and four German Cups. He was top scorer in Germany a record seven times and scored a then record 85 goals in the year of 1972. For Germany, he scored 68 times in 62 caps, winning the 1972 European Championship and 1974 World Cup.

FIFA
Ballon d'Or
Previous
Winners

GIANNI RIVERA
Position: Midfielder
Birth date: August 18, 1943
Birth place: Alessandria, Italy
Height: 1.75m (5ft 9in)
Clubs: Alessandria, AC Milan
International: Italy
Ballon d'Or wins: 1 (1969)

Before the likes of Francesco Totti and Roberto Baggio, Rivera was the original Italian playmaker. After impressing as a 16-year-old for hometown club Alessandria, the creative midfielder made the move to AC Milan. He spent the rest of his career at the San Siro, racking up 658 games in 19 seasons. The pinpoint passer won 12 honours including two European Cups and four Serie A titles. He also helped Italy win the 1968 European Championship and reach the 1970 World Cup final where the Azzurri lost 4-1 to Brazil.

GEORGE BEST
Position: Winger
Birth date: May 22, 1946
Birth place: Belfast, Northern Ireland
Height: 1.75m (5ft 9in)
Clubs: Manchester United, Jewish Guild (loan), Dunstable Town (loan), Stockport County, Cork Celtic, Los Angeles Aztecs, Fulham, Fort Lauderdale Strikers, Hibernian, San Jose Earthquakes, Sea Bee, Hong Kong Rangers, Bournemouth, Brisbane Lions, Osborne Park Galeb, Nuneaton Borough, Tobermore United
International: Northern Ireland
Ballon d'Or wins: 1 (1968)

Described as the best player to have never graced a major tournament, Best was a magician and undoubtedly one of the greatest players to have graced a football pitch. The Northern Ireland star was regarded as the 'Fifth Beatle' as he became the first fully fledged celebrity footballer. On the pitch, the wing wizard scored 184 times in 474 games for Manchester United and famously struck the second goal in the club's 1968 European Cup final win against Benfica. He represented his country 37 times in 13 years and was even considered for the 1982 World Cup at the age of 36.

FLORIAN ALBERT

Position: Forward
Birth date: September 15, 1941
Birth place: Budapest, Hungary
Height: 1.81m (5ft 11in)
Clubs: Ferencvaros , Hungary
International: Hungary
Ballon d'Or wins: 1 (1967)

Ferenc Puskas is the greatest Hungarian footballer of all time, but Florian Albert isn't too far behind him. He spent his whole career with Ferencvaros where he scored twice on his debut at just 17 years of age. The attacker's impressive tally of 255 league goals in 351 games helped the club to four league titles. On the international stage, the deadly finisher hit the net 31 times in 75 games and he was the joint top scorer at the 1962 World Cup.

BOBBY CHARLTON

Position: Forward
Birth date: October 11, 1937
Birth place: Ashington, Northumberland, England
Clubs: Manchester United, Preston North End, Waterford United
International: England
Ballon d'Or wins: 1 (1966)

Charlton spent the majority of his career with Manchester United, scoring a still club-record 249 goals in 758 appearances. A survivor of the 1958 Munich air disaster, which saw 20 people lose their lives, the attacker helped the club recover from the tragedy by winning three league titles, FA Cup and the European Cup. The year Charlton was recognised as the world's best also saw him help England win the 1966 World Cup. He played at five major tournaments and is still the Three Lions' record scorer with 49 goals in 109 caps.

FIFA
Ballon d'Or
Previous Winners

EUSEBIO
Position: Forward
Birth date: January 25, 1942
Birth place: Lisbon, Portugal
Height: 1.75m (5ft 9in)
Clubs: Sporting de Lourenco Marques, Benfica, Boston Minutemen, Monterrey, Toronto Metros-Croatia, Beira-Mar, Las Vegas Quicksilvers, Uniao de Tomar, New Jersey Americans
International: Portugal
Ballon d'Or wins: 1 (1965)

Nicknamed the Black Panther, the Black Pearl or simply The King, Eusebio was one of the world's first footballing superstars and is one of the greatest to play for Portugal. Born in Mozambique, a Portuguese colony until 1975, the fearless forward moved to Benfica at the age of 18. He notched up a club-record 474 goals in 440 matches and won 18 major trophies, including back-to-back European Cups in 1961 and 1962. For Portugal, Eusebio hit the net 41 times in 61 caps and was the top scorer at the 1966 World Cup.

DENIS LAW
Position: Striker
Birth date: February 24, 1940
Birth place: Aberdeen, Scotland
Height: 1.75m (5ft 9in)
Clubs: Huddersfield Town, Manchester City, Torino, Manchester United
International: Scotland
Ballon d'Or wins: 1 (1964)

The only Scot to have won the award, Denis Law is one of the greatest goalscorers Britain has ever seen. After previously playing for Manchester City, a less successful year in Italy saw him return to England with Manchester United, for a then British transfer fee of £115,000, in what would prove to be one of the greatest buys in history. In 11 seasons at Old Trafford, Law scored 237 goals in 404 appearances, won two league titles, the FA Cup and 1968 European Cup, but missed the final against Benfica through injury.

LEV YASHIN
Position: Goalkeeper
Birth date: October 22, 1929
Birth place: Moscow, Soviet Union
Height: 1.89m (6ft 2in)
Clubs: Dynamo Moscow
International: Soviet Union
Ballon d'Or wins: 1 (1963)

The Moscow born star was known as The Black Spider due to his amazing reflexes which saw him save over 150 penalties and keep 270 clean sheets in his career. He's the only goalkeeper to have won the Ballon d'Or and is regarded by many as the greatest stopper of the 20th century. He spent the whole of his 20 year-career with Dynamo Moscow, winning eight major honours. For the Soviet Union, the super stopper won the 1960 European Championship.

JOSEF MASOPUST
Position: Midfielder
Birth date: February 9, 1931
Birth place: Strimice, Czechoslovakia
Height: 1.77m (5ft 9in)
Clubs: ZSJ Technomat Teplice, Dukla Prague, Crossing Molenbeek
International: Czechoslovakia
Ballon d'Or wins: 1 (1962)

The midfield maestro was awarded the Ballon d'Or in 1962 after his brilliant performances helped Czechoslovakia reach the World Cup final where he scored the opening goal in a 3-1 defeat to Brazil. Masopust, who played in three major tournaments, scored 10 times in 63 caps for his country. Sixteen of the pass master's 20-year professional career were spent with Dukla Prague where he struck 79 times in 386 games and won eight Czechoslovakian Football League Championships.

FIFA
Ballon d'Or
Previous
Winners

OMAR SIVORI

Position: Forward
Birth date: October 2, 1935
Birth place: San Nicholas, Argentina
Height: 1.63m (5ft 4in)
Clubs: River Plate, Juventus, Napoli
International: Argentina, Italy
Ballon d'Or wins: 1 (1961)

After impressing as a youngster at River Plate, Sivori was picked up by Juventus. It was in Turin where the tricky attacker made his name, scoring 167 times in 253 appearances. He won three Serie A titles and two Italian Cups in his eight years at the club, and is still the only Juve player to have scored six goals in a game by netting a dozen times in a 9-1 win over Inter Milan in 1961. Sivori originally represented Argentina, scoring nine times in 19 caps and winning the Copa America before he was banned from playing for them by the Italian government.

LUIS SUAREZ

Position: Midfielder
Birth date: May 2, 1935
Birth place: A Coruna, Galicia, Spain
Height: 1.75m (5ft 9in)
Clubs: Deportivo La Coruna, Espana Industrial, Barcelona, Internazionale, Sampdoria
International: Spain
Ballon d'Or wins: 1 (1960)

The award's first Spanish recipient, Suarez was a deep-lying midfielder who would dictate and create from just in front of his defenders. He shone at Barcelona, helping a talented side to two La Liga titles, two Copa del Reys and two Fairs Cups in six years. A world record £142,000 transfer to Internazionale in 1961 led to more honours for the man that helped secure Spain's first international trophy by winning the 1964 European Championship. The A Coruna-born star scored 14 times in 32 games for his country.

FIFA
Ballon d'Or
Previous Winners

ALFREDO DI STEFANO

Position: Forward
Birth date: July 4, 1926
Birth place: Buenos Aires, Argentina
Height: 1.78m (5ft 10in)
Clubs: River Plate, Huracan (loan), Millonarios, Real Madrid, Espanyol
International: Argentina, Colombia, Spain
Ballon d'Or wins: 2 (1959, 1957)

The man recognised as the fourth best player of the 20th century behind Pele, Diego Maradona and Franz Beckenbauer, Di Stefano was the first player to win the award twice. Despite playing for three different nations (Argentina, Colombia and Spain) he never played in the World Cup finals but did win the 1947 Copa America trophy with Argentina. The powerful forward had an incredibly successful career at club level, winning five European Cups with Real Madrid and scoring 485 goals.

RAYMOND KOPA

Position: Midfielder
Birth date: October 13, 1931
Birth place: Noeux-les-Mines, France
Height: 1.69m (5ft 6in)
Clubs: Angers, Stade Reims, Real Madrid
International: France
Ballon d'Or wins: 1 (1958)

The second winner of the award, Kopa was an integral part of the French national team in the 1950s. He helped his country finish third in the 1958 World Cup where he won the Golden Ball for being voted the tournament's best player. After five successful years with Stade Reims, which brought five league titles, the attacking midfielder moved to Real Madrid. In Spain, he won three consecutive European Cups, becoming the first Frenchman to win the competition. The playmaker also won two Spanish league titles.

STANLEY MATTHEWS

Position: Winger
Birth date: February 1, 1937
Birth place: Hanley, Stoke-on-Trent, England
Clubs: Stoke City, Blackpool
International: England
Ballon d'Or wins: 1 (1956)

After spending 15 years with boyhood club Stoke City, Matthews spent 14 seasons with Blackpool where he became the inaugural winner of the Ballon d'Or in 1956. He lifted the FA Cup with the Lancashire side before returning to play out the last four years of his career at Stoke where he had earlier won two Second Division titles. The silky wide man, who is the only player to be knighted while still playing, turned out at the top level until he was 50 years old. He is still the oldest player to have represented England (42) and he won nine British Home Championships.

FIFA FIFPro
World XI

Since 2005, FIFPro (International Federation of Professional Footballers) has invited all professional footballers to vote for their team of the year.

Each player is required to choose one goalkeeper, four defenders, three midfielders and three strikers.

In 2008 FIFPro joined forces with FIFA, which changed the team's name from the FIFPro World XI to the FIFA FIFPro World XI

The team is named each January at FIFA's Ballon d'Or ceremony.

Here's a rundown of all the World XIs.

FIFA FIFPro World XI 2005

Goalkeeper

Dida,
AC Milan & Brazil

Defenders

Cafu
AC Milan & Brazil

Alessandro Nesta
AC Milan & Italy

Paolo Maldini
AC Milan & Italy

John Terry
Chelsea & England

Midfielders

Frank Lampard
Chelsea & England

Claude Makelele
Chelsea & France

Zinedine Zidane
Real Madrid & France

Ronaldinho
Barcelona & Brazil

Strikers

Samuel Eto'o
Barcelona & Cameroon

Andriy Shevchenko
AC Milan & Ukraine

Goalkeeper

Gianluigi Buffon
Juventus & Italy

FIFA FIFPro World XI 2006

Defenders

Fabio Cannavaro
Juventus/Real Madrid & Italy

Lilian Thuram
Juventus/Barcelona & France

Gianluca Zambrotta
Juventus/Barcelona & Italy

John Terry
Chelsea & England

Midfielders

Andrea Pirlo
AC Milan & Italy

Kaka
AC Milan & Brazil

Zinedine Zidane
Real Madrid & France

Strikers

Samuel Eto'o
Barcelona & Cameroon

Ronaldinho
Barcelona & Brazil

Thierry Henry
Arsenal & France

FIFA FIFPro World XI 2007

Goalkeeper

Gianluigi Buffon
Juventus & Italy

Defenders

Fabio Cannavaro
Real Madrid & Italy

Alessandro Nesta
AC Milan & Italy

Carles Puyol
Barcelona & Spain

John Terry
Chelsea & England

Midfielders

Steven Gerrard
Liverpool & England

Kaka
AC Milan & Brazil

Cristiano Ronaldo
Man United & Portugal

Strikers

Lionel Messi
Barcelona & Argentina

Ronaldinho
Barcelona & Brazil

Didier Drogba
Chelsea & Ivory Coast

Goalkeeper

Iker Casillas
Real Madrid & Spain

Defenders

Carles Puyol
Barcelona & Spain

John Terry
Chelsea & England

Rio Ferdinand
Man United & England

Sergio Ramos
Real Madrid & Spain

Midfielders

Steven Gerrard
Liverpool & England

Xavi Hernandez
Barcelona & Spain

Kaka
AC Milan & Brazil

Strikers

Lionel Messi
Barcelona & Argentina

Fernando Torres
Liverpool & Spain

Cristiano Ronaldo
Man United & Portugal

FIFA
FIFPro
World XI
2009

Goalkeeper

Iker Casillas
Real Madrid & Spain

Defenders

Dani Alves
Barcelona & Brazil

John Terry
Chelsea & England

Nemanja Vidic
Man United & Serbia

Patrice Evra
Man United & France

Midfielders

Steven Gerrard
Liverpool & England

Xavi Hernandez
Barcelona & Spain

Andres Iniesta
Barcelona & Spain

Strikers

Lionel Messi
Barcelona & Argentina

Fernando Torres
Liverpool & Spain

Cristiano Ronaldo
Man United/Real Madrid
& Portugal

Goalkeeper

Iker Casillas
Real Madrid & Spain

Defenders

Maicon
Internazionale & Brazil

Gerard Pique
Barcelona & Spain

Carles Puyol
Barcelona & Spain

Lucio
Internazionale & Brazil

Midfielders

Wesley Sneijder
Internazionale & Netherlands

Xavi Hernandez
Barcelona & Spain

Andres Iniesta
Barcelona & Spain

Strikers

Lionel Messi
Barcelona & Argentina

David Villa
Barcelona & Spain

Cristiano Ronaldo
Real Madrid & Portugal

FIFA
FIFPro
World XI
2011

Goalkeeper

Iker Casillas
Real Madrid & Spain

Defenders

Dani Alves
Barcelona & Brazil

Gerard Pique
Barcelona & Spain

Sergio Ramos
Real Madrid & Spain

Nemanja Vidic
Man United & Serbia

Midfielders

Xabi Alonso
Real Madrid & Spain

Xavi Hernandez
Barcelona & Spain

Andres Iniesta
Barcelona & Spain

Strikers

Lionel Messi
Barcelona & Argentina

Wayne Rooney
Man United & England

Cristiano Ronaldo
Real Madrid & Portugal

FIFA FIFPro World XI 2012

Goalkeeper

Iker Casillas
Real Madrid & Spain

Defenders

Dani Alves
Barcelona & Brazil

Gerard Pique
Barcelona & Spain

Sergio Ramos
Real Madrid & Spain

Marcelo
Real Madrid & Brazil

Midfielders

Xabi Alonso
Real Madrid & Spain

Xavi Hernandez
Barcelona & Spain

Andres Iniesta
Barcelona & Spain

Strikers

Lionel Messi
Barcelona & Argentina

Radamel Falcao
Atletico Madrid & Colombia

Cristiano Ronaldo
Real Madrid & Portugal

FIFA
FIFPro
World XI
2013

Goalkeeper

Manuel Neuer
Bayern Munich & Germany

Defenders

Dani Alves
Barcelona & Brazil

Thiago Silva
Paris Saint-Germain
& Brazil

Sergio Ramos
Real Madrid & Spain

Philipp Lahm
Bayern Munich & Germany

Midfielders

Franck Ribery
Bayern Munich & France

Xavi Hernandez
Barcelona & Spain

Andres Iniesta
Barcelona & Spain

Strikers

Lionel Messi
Barcelona & Argentina

Zlatan Ibrahimovic
Paris Saint-Germain
& Sweden

Cristiano Ronaldo
Real Madrid & Portugal

TOP APPEARANCES

7 APPEARANCES

Lionel Messi
Country: Argentina
Years: 2007, 2008, 2009, 2010, 2011, 2012, 2013

Cristiano Ronaldo
Country: Portugal
Years: 2007, 2008, 2009, 2010, 2011, 2012, 2013

6 APPEARANCES

Xavi Hernandez
Country: Spain
Years: 2008, 2009, 2010, 2011, 2012, 2013

5 APPEARANCES

Andres Iniesta
Country: Spain
Years: 2009, 2010, 2011, 2012, 2013

Iker Casillas
Country: Spain
Years: 2008, 2009, 2010, 2011, 2012

John Terry
Country: England
Years: 2005, 2006, 2007, 2008, 2009

4 APPEARANCES

Sergio Ramos
Country: Spain
Years: 2008, 2011, 2012, 2013

Dani Alves
Country: Brazil
Years: 2009, 2011, 2012, 2013

3 APPEARANCES

Steven Gerrard
Country: England
Years: 2007, 2008, 2009

Kaka
Country: Brazil
Years: 2006, 2007, 2008

Gerard Pique
Country: Spain
Years: 2010, 2011, 2012

Carles Puyol
Country: Spain
Years: 2007, 2008, 2010

Ronaldinho
Country: Brazil
Years: 2005, 2006, 2007

BY CLUB

1st

Barcelona

Appearances - 36: Lionel Messi (7), Xavi Hernandez (6), Andres Iniesta (5), Dani Alves (4), Gerard Pique, Carles Puyol, Ronaldinho (3), Samuel Eto'o (2), Lilian Thuram, David Villa, Gianluca Zambrotta (1)

2nd

Real Madrid

Appearances - 21: Cristiano Ronaldo, Iker Casillas (5), Sergio Ramos (4), Xabi Alonso, Fabio Cannavaro, Zinedine Zidane (2), Marcelo (1)

3rd

AC Milan

Appearances - 10: Kaka (3), Alessandro Nesta (2), Cafu, Dida, Paolo Maldini, Andrea Pirlo, Andriy Shevchenko (1)

4th

Chelsea

Appearances - 8: John Terry (5), Didier Drogba, Claude Makelele, Frank Lampard (1)

Manchester United

Appearances - 8: Cristiano Ronaldo (3), Nemanja Vidic (2), Patrice Evra, Rio Ferdinand, Wayne Rooney (1)

6th

Juventus

Appearances - 5: Gianluigi Buffon (2), Fabio Cannavaro, Lilian Thuram, Gianluca Zambrotta (1)

Liverpool

Appearances - 5: Steven Gerrard (3), Fernando Torres (2)

8th

Bayern Munich

Appearances - 3: Philipp Lahm, Manuel Neuer, Franck Ribery (1)

Internazionale

Appearances - 3: Lucio, Maicon, Wesley Sneijder (1)

10th

Paris Saint-Germain

Appearances - 2: Zlatan Ibrahimovic, Thiago Silva (1)

BY NATIONALITY

1st

Spain
Appearances - 31: Xavi Hernandez (6), Iker Casillas, Andres Iniesta (5), Sergio Ramos (4), Gerard Pique, Carles Puyol (3), Fernando Torres, Xabi Alonso (2), David Villa (1)

2nd

Brazil
Appearances - 16: Dani Alves (4), Kaka, Ronaldinho (3), Cafu, Lucio, Maicon, Marcelo, Thiago Silva, Dida (1)

3rd

England
Appearances - 11: John Terry (5), Steven Gerrard (3), Rio Ferdinand, Frank Lampard, Wayne Rooney (1)

4th

Italy
Appearances - 9: Gianluigi Buffon, Fabio Cannavaro, Alessandro Nesta (2), Paolo Maldini, Andrea Pirlo, Gianluca Zambrotta (1)

5th

Argentina
Appearances - 7: Lionel Messi (7)

France
Appearances - 7: Zinedine Zidane (2), Patrice Evra, Thierry Henry, Claude Makelele, Franck Ribery, Lilian Thuram (1)

Portugal
Appearances - 7: Cristiano Ronaldo (7)

8th

Cameroon
Appearances - 2: Samuel Eto'o (2)

Germany
Appearances - 2: Manuel Neuer, Philipp Lahm (1)

Serbia
Appearances - 2: Nemanja Vidic (2)

BY LEAGUE

1st
La Liga: 58

2nd
Premier League: 22

3rd
Serie A: 18

4th
Bundesliga: 3

5th
Ligue 1: 2

UEFA TEAM
AND BEST PLAYER IN
EUROPE AWARD

The UEFA Team of the Year is unique in the fact the 11 players are voted for by fans through UEFA's official website.

The award, first started in 2001, is revealed in January of each year. Until 2011, 60 players and coaches were shortlisted but in 2012 this changed to a total of 40 players (4 goalkeepers, 12 defenders, 12 midfielders and 12 forwards) while the best coach award was scrapped.

The UEFA Best Player in Europe Award, initially known as the UEFA Club Footballer of the Year Award, was introduced in 1998 and is handed to the individual considered the best throughout the previous season.

Fifty-three sports journalists vote for their initial top-three players which results in a three-man shortlist. The same journalists then take another vote to decide who wins the prestigious award.

Here's UEFA's Best Player in Europe winners and Teams of the Year.

UEFA's CLUB FOOTBALLER OF THE YEAR

1998
Ronaldo
Position: Striker
Club: Inter Milan
Country: Brazil

1999
David Beckham
Position: Midfielder
Club: Manchester United
Country: England

2000
Fernando Redondo
Position: Midfielder
Club: Real Madrid
Country: Argentina

2001
Stefan Effenberg
Position: Midfielder
Club: Bayern Munich
Country: Germany

2002
Zinedine Zidane
Position: Midfielder
Club: Real Madrid
Country: France

2003
Gianluigi Buffon
Position: Goalkeeper
Club: Juventus
Country: Italy

2004
Deco
Position: Midfielder
Club: FC Porto
Country: Portugal

2005
Steven Gerrard
Position: Midfielder
Club: Liverpool
Country: England

2006
Ronaldinho
Position: Forward
Club: Barcelona
Country: Brazil

2007
Kaka
Position: Midfielder
Club: AC Milan
Country: Brazil

2008
Cristiano Ronaldo
Position: Forward
Club: Manchester United
Country: Portugal

2009
Lionel Messi
Position: Forward
Club: Barcelona
Country: Argentina

2010
Diego Militio
Position: Striker
Club: Inter Milan
Country: Argentina

UEFA BEST PLAYER IN EUROPE

2011
Lionel Messi
Position: Forward
Club: Barcelona
Country: Argentina

2012
Andres Iniesta
Position: Midfielder
Club: Barcelona
Country: Spain

2013
Franck Ribery
Position: Midfielder
Club: Bayern Munich
Country: France

BY CLUB

1st

Barcelona
Winners - 4: Lionel Messi (2), Ronaldinho, Andres Iniesta

2nd

Bayern Munich
Winners - 2: Stefan Effenberg, Franck Ribery

Inter Milan
Winners - 2: Diego Militio, Ronaldo

Manchester United
Winners - 2: David Beckham, Cristiano Ronaldo

Real Madrid
Winners - 2: Fernando Redondo, Zinedine Zidane

6th

Juventus
Winners - 1: Gianluigi Buffon

FC Porto
Winners - 1: Deco

Liverpool
Winners - 1: Steven Gerrard

AC Milan
Winners - 1: Kaka

BY NATIONALITY

1st

Argentina
Winners - 4: Lionel Messi (2), Fernando Redondo, Diego Militio

2nd

Brazil
Winners - 3: Ronaldo, Ronaldinho, Kaka

3rd

England
Winners - 2: David Beckham. Steven Gerrard

France
Winners - 2: Zinedine Zidane, Franck Ribery

Portugal
Winners - 2: Deco, Cristiano Ronaldo

6th

Germany
Winners - 1: Stefen Effenberg

Italy
Winners - 1: Gianluigi Buffon

Spain
Winners - 1: Andres Iniesta

BY LEAGUE

1st	2nd	3rd	4th	5th
La Liga: 6	Serie A: 4	Premier League: 3	Bundesliga: 2	Primeira Liga: 1

UEFA
BEST TEAM IN EUROPE AWARD
2001

Goalkeeper

Santiago Canizares
Valencia & Spain

Defenders

Cosmin Contra
Alaves/AC Milan
& Romania

Sami Hyypia
Liverpool & Finland

Patrik Andersson
Bayern Munich/Barcelona
& Sweden

Bixente Lizarazu
Bayern Munich & France

Midfielders

Kily Gonzalez
Valencia & Argentina

Zinedine Zidane
Juventus/Real Madrid
& France

Patrick Vieira
Arsenal & France

David Beckham
Manchester United
& England

Strikers

Thierry Henry
Arsenal & France

David Trezeguet
Juventus & France

Coach
Gerard Houllier
Liverpool

Goalkeeper

Rustu Recber
Fenerbache & Turkey

Defenders

Alessandro Nesta
Lazio/AC Milan & Italy

Carles Puyol
Barcelona & Spain

Christian Chivu
Ajax & Romania

Roberto Carlos
Real Madrid & Brazil

Midfielders

Clarence Seedorf
Internazionale/AC Milan
& Netherlands

Zinedine Zidane
Real Madrid & France

Michael Ballack
Bayer Leverkusen/
Bayern Munich & Germany

Damien Duff
Blackburn Rovers &
Republic of Ireland

Strikers

Thierry Henry
Arsenal & France

Ronaldo
Internazionale/Real Madrid
& Brazil

Coach
Senol Gunes
Turkey

UEFA BEST TEAM IN EUROPE AWARD 2003

Goalkeeper

Gianluigi Buffon
Juventus & Italy

Defenders

Paulo Ferreira
Porto & Portugal

Alessandro Nesta
AC Milan & Italy

Paolo Maldini
AC Milan & Italy

Roberto Carlos
Real Madrid & Brazil

Midfielders

Pavel Nedved
Juventus & Czech Republic

Zinedine Zidane
Real Madrid & France

Luis Figo
Real Madrid & Portugal

David Beckham
Manchester United/ Real Madrid & England

Strikers

Thierry Henry
Arsenal & France

Ruud van Nistelrooy
Manchester United & Netherlands

Coach

Jose Mourinho
FC Porto

Goalkeeper

Gianluigi Buffon
Juventus & Italy

Defenders

Cafu
AC Milan & Brazil

Alessandro Nesta
AC Milan & Italy

Ricardo Carvalho
Porto/Chelsea & Portugal

Ashley Cole
Chelsea & England

Midfielders

Pavel Nedved
Juventus &
Czech Republic

Maniche
Porto & Portugal

Cristiano Ronaldo
Manchester United
& Portugal

Ronaldinho
Barcelona & Brazil

Strikers

Thierry Henry
Arsenal & France

Andriy Shevchenko
AC Milan & Ukraine

Coach
José Mourinho
FC Porto/Chelsea

UEFA BEST TEAM IN EUROPE AWARD 2005

Goalkeeper

Petr Cech
Chelsea &
Czech Republic

Defenders

Cafu
AC Milan & Brazil

Paolo Maldini
AC Milan & Italy

Carles Puyol
Barcelona & Spain

John Terry
Chelsea & England

Midfielders

Luis Garcia
Liverpool & Spain

Steven Gerrard
Liverpool & England

Pavel Nedved
Juventus &
Czech Republic

Ronaldinho
Barcelona & Brazil

Strikers

Samuel Eto'o
Barcelona & Cameroon

Andriy Shevchenko
AC Milan & Ukraine

Coach

José Mourinho
Chelsea

Goalkeeper

Gianluigi Buffon
Juventus & Italy

Defenders

Fabio Cannavaro
Juventus/Real Madrid
& Italy

Carles Puyol
Barcelona & Spain

Gianluca Zambrotta
Juventus/Barcelona & Italy

Philipp Lahm
Bayern Munich
& Germany

Midfielders

Ronaldinho
Barcelona & Brazil

Kaka
AC Milan & Brazil

Steven Gerrard
Liverpool & England

Cesc Fabregas
Arsenal & Spain

Strikers

Samuel Eto'o
Barcelona & Cameroon

Thierry Henry
Arsenal & France

Coach

Frank Rijkaard
Barcelona

Goalkeeper

Iker Casillas
Real Madrid & Spain

Defenders

Dani Alves
Sevilla & Brazil

Alessandro Nesta
AC Milan & Italy

Eric Abidal
Lyon/Barcelona & France

John Terry
Chelsea & England

Midfielders

Steven Gerrard
Liverpool & England

Kaka
AC Milan & Brazil

Cristiano Ronaldo
Manchester United
& Portugal

Clarence Seedorf
AC Milan & Netherlands

Strikers

Didier Drogba
Chelsea & Ivory Coast

Zlatan Ibrahimovic
Internazionale & Sweden

Coach

Sir Alex Ferguson
Manchester United

Goalkeeper

Iker Casillas
Real Madrid & Spain

Defenders

Carles Puyol
Barcelona & Spain

John Terry
Chelsea & England

Philipp Lahm
Bayern Munich & Germany

Sergio Ramos
Real Madrid & Spain

Midfielders

Cesc Fabregas
Arsenal & Spain

Xavi Hernandez
Barcelona & Spain

Franck Ribery
Bayern Munich & France

Cristiano Ronaldo
Manchester United & Portugal

Strikers

Lionel Messi
Barcelona & Argentina

Fernando Torres
Liverpool & Spain

Coach
Sir Alex Ferguson
Manchester United

UEFA BEST TEAM IN EUROPE AWARD 2009

Goalkeeper

Iker Casillas
Real Madrid & Spain

Defenders

Dani Alves
Barcelona & Brazil

John Terry
Chelsea & England

Carles Puyol
Barcelona & Spain

Patrice Evra
Manchester United
& France

Midfielders

Kaka
AC Milan/Real Madrid
& Brazil

Xavi Hernandez
Barcelona & Spain

Andres Iniesta
Barcelona & Spain

Cristiano Ronaldo
Manchester United/
Real Madrid & Portugal

Strikers

Lionel Messi
Barcelona & Argentina

Zlatan Ibrahimovic
Internazionale/Barcelona
& Sweden

Coach

Pep Guardiola
Barcelona

Goalkeeper

Iker Casillas
Real Madrid & Spain

UEFA
BEST TEAM
IN EUROPE
AWARD
2010

Defenders

Maicon
Internazionale & Brazil

Gerard Pique
Barcelona & Spain

Carles Puyol
Barcelona & Spain

Ashley Cole
Chelsea & England

Midfielders

Wesley Sneijder
Internazionale &
Netherlands

Xavi Hernandez
Barcelona & Spain

Andres Iniesta
Barcelona & Spain

Cristiano Ronaldo
Real Madrid & Portugal

Strikers

Lionel Messi
Barcelona & Argentina

David Villa
Valencia/Barcelona
& Spain

Coach
Jose Mourinho
Internazionale/Real Madrid

UEFA BEST TEAM IN EUROPE AWARD 2011

Goalkeeper

Iker Casillas
Real Madrid & Spain

Defenders

Dani Alves
Barcelona & Brazil

Gerard Pique
Barcelona & Spain

Thiago Silva
AC Milan & Brazil

Marcelo
Real Madrid & Brazil

Midfielders

Arjen Robben
Bayern Munich & Netherlands

Xavi Hernandez
Barcelona & Spain

Andres Iniesta
Barcelona & Spain

Gareth Bale
Tottenham Hotspur & Wales

Strikers

Lionel Messi
Barcelona & Argentina

Cristiano Ronaldo
Real Madrid & Portugal

Goalkeeper

Iker Casillas
Real Madrid & Spain

Defenders

Philipp Lahm
Bayern Munich & Germany

Gerard Pique
Barcelona & Spain

Sergio Ramos
Real Madrid & Spain

Thiago Silva
AC Milan/Paris Saint-
Germain & Brazil

Midfielders

Andrea Pirlo
Juventus & Italy

Xavi Hernandez
Barcelona & Spain

Andres Iniesta
Barcelona & Spain

Mesut Ozil
Real Madrid & Germany

Strikers

Lionel Messi
Barcelona & Argentina

Cristiano Ronaldo
Real Madrid & Portugal

UEFA BEST TEAM IN EUROPE AWARD 2013

Goalkeeper

Manuel Neuer
Bayern Munich & Germany

Defenders

David Alaba
Bayern Munich & Austria

Thiago Silva
Paris Saint-Germain & Brazil

Sergio Ramos
Real Madrid & Spain

Philipp Lahm
Bayern Munich & Germany

Midfielders

Franck Ribery
Bayern Munich & France

Gareth Bale
Tottenham Hotspur/ Real Madrid & Wales

Mesut Ozil
Real Madrid/Arsenal & Germany

Marco Reus
Borussia Dortmund & Germany

Strikers

Zlatan Ibrahimovic
Paris Saint-Germain & Sweden

Cristiano Ronaldo
Real Madrid & Portugal

TOP APPEARANCES

8 APPEARANCES

Cristiano Ronaldo
Country: Portugal
Years: 2004, 2007, 2008, 2009, 2010, 2011, 2012, 2013

6 APPEARANCES

Carles Puyol
Country: Spain
Years: 2002, 2005, 2006, 2008, 2009, 2010

Iker Casillas
Country: Spain
Years: 2007, 2008, 2009, 2010, 2011, 2012

5 APPEARANCES

Thierry Henry
Country: France
Years: 2001, 2002, 2003, 2004, 2006

Xavi Hernandez
Country: Spain
Years: 2008, 2009, 2010, 2011, 2012

Lionel Messi
Country: Argentina
Years: 2008, 2009, 2010, 2011, 2012

4 APPEARANCES

John Terry
Country: England
Years: 2005, 2007, 2008, 2009

Andres Iniesta
Country: Spain
Years: 2009, 2010, 2011, 2012

Alessandro Nesta
Country: Italy
Years: 2002, 2003, 2004, 2007

Philipp Lahm
Country: Germany
Years: 2006, 2008, 2012, 2013

3 11 players

2 13 players

1 32 players

BY CLUB

1st

Barcelona
Appearances - 37: Carles Puyol (6), Xavi Hernandez, Lionel Messi (5), Andres Iniesta (4), Ronaldinho, Gerard Pique (3) Dani Alves, Samuel Eto'o (2), Eric Abidal, Zlatan Ibrahimovic, Patrik Andersson, Gianluca Zambrotta, David Villa, Pep Guardiola, Frank Rijkaard (1)

2nd

Real Madrid
Appearances - 29: Iker Casillas (6), Cristiano Ronaldo (5), Sergio Ramos, Zinedine Zidane (3), Mesut Ozil, Roberto Carlos (2), Kaka, Fabio Cannavaro, David Beckham, Luis Figo, Ronaldo, Gareth Bale, Marcelo, Jose Mourinho (1)

3rd

AC Milan
Appearances - 18: Alessandro Nesta (4), Kaka (3), Clarence Seedorf, Cafu, Paolo Maldini, Thiago Silva, Andriy Shevchenko (2), Cosmin Contra(1)

4th

Bayern Munich
Appearances - 12: Philipp Lahm (4), Franck Ribery (2), Arjen Robben, David Alaba, Manuel Neuer, Michael Ballack, Patrick Andersson, Bixente Lizarazu (1)

5th

Juventus
Appearances - 11: Pavel Nedved, Gianluigi Buffon (3), Andrea Pirlo, Fabio Cannavaro, Zinedine Zidane, Gianluca Zambrotta, David Trezeguet (1)

6th

Arsenal
Appearances - 10: Thierry Henry (5), Cesc Fabregas (2), Mesut Ozil, Patrick Vieira, Ashley Cole (1)

Chelsea
Appearances - 10: John Terry (4), Jose Mourinho (2), Didier Drogba, Ashley Cole, Ricardo Carvalho, Petr Cech (1)

Manchester United
Appearances - 10: Cristiano Ronaldo (4), Sir Alex Ferguson, David Beckham (2), Patrice Evra, Ruud van Nistelrooy (1)

9th

Internazionale
Appearances - 7: Zlatan Ibrahimovic (2), Maicon, Wesley Sneijder, Clarence Seedorf, Ronaldo, Jose Mourinho (1)

Liverpool
Appearances - 7: Steven Gerrard (3), Fernando Torres, Luis Garcia, Sami Hyypia, Gerard Houllier (1)

5	3	2	1
1 club FC Porto	2 clubs Paris Saint-Germain, Valencia	1 club Tottenham Hostspur	9 clubs

BY NATIONALITY

1st

Spain

Appearances - 34: Carles Puyol, Iker Casillas (6), Xavi Hernandez (5), Andres Iniesta (4), Sergio Ramos, Gerard Pique, (3), Cesc Fabregas (2), Fernando Torres, David Villa, Luis Garcia, Santiago Canizares, Pep Guardiola (1)

2nd

Brazil

Appearances - 19: Dani Alves, Kaka, Ronaldinho, Thiago Silva (3), Cafu, Roberto Carlos (2), Ronaldo, Marcelo, Maicon (1)

3rd

France

Appearances - 16: Thierry Henry (5), Zinedine Zidane (3), Franck Ribery (2), Patrice Evra, Eric Abidal, David Trezeguet, Bixente Lizarazu, Patrick Vieira, Gerard Houllier (1)

Portugal

Appearances - 16:
Cristiano Ronaldo (8), Jose Mourinho (4), Luis Figo, Maniche, Ricardo Carvalho, Paulo Ferreira (1)

5th

Italy

Appearances - 12:
Alessandro Nesta (4), Gianluigi Buffon (3), Paolo Maldini (2), Andrea Pirlo, Fabio Cannavaro, Gianluca Zambrotta (1)

6th

England

Appearances - 11:
John Terry (4), Steven Gerrard (3), David Beckham, Ashley Cole (2)

7th

Germany

Appearances - 9: Philipp Lahm (4), Mesut Ozil (2), Michael Ballack, Manuel Neuer, Marco Reus (1)

8th

Argentina

Appearances - 6: Lionel Messi (5), Kily Gonzalez (1)

Netherlands

Appearances - 6: Clarence Seedorf (2), Wesley Sneijder, Ruud van Nistelrooy, Arjen Robben, Frank Rijkaard (1)

BY LEAGUE

1st La Liga: 71

2nd Premier League: 40

3rd Serie A: 37

4th Bundesliga: 14

5th Ligue 1: 4

Primeira Liga: 4

7th Eredivisie: 1

Super Lig; 1

PFA
AWARDS

The Professional Footballers' Association (PFA) was established in 1907 to act as the trade union for professional footballers in England and Wales.

Andy Gray, Aston Villa

In 1974, the PFA came up with four awards - the Players' Player of the Year, Young Player of the Year, Team of the Year and the Merit Award, which is given to the person who's contributed the most over a season.

These awards, which have seen many prestigious world-class players honoured, are handed out at a ceremony every April.

Leeds United's Norman Hunter was the first to collect the Player of the Year Award while Liverpool's Luis Suarez is the most recent recipient.

Three players, Andy Gray of Aston Villa (1977), Manchester United's Cristiano Ronaldo (2007) and Tottenham Hotspur's Gareth Bale (2013), are the only three players to have won both the Player and Young Player of the Year Awards in the same year.

Here's a look at all the PFA winners.

Gareth Bale,
Tottenham Hotspur

Cristiano Ronaldo,
Manchester United

PLAYER OF THE YEAR

1974 - NORMAN HUNTER
Leeds United

1975 - COLIN TODD
Derby County

1976 - PAT JENNINGS
Tottenham Hotspur

1977 - ANDY GRAY
Aston Villa

1978 - PETER SHILTON
Nottingham Forest

1979 - LIAM BRADY
Arsenal

1980 - TERRY MCDERMOTT
Liverpool

1981 - JOHN WARK
Ipswich Town

1982 - KEVIN KEEGAN
Southampton

1983 - KENNY DALGLISH
Liverpool

1984 - IAN RUSH
Liverpool

1985 - PETER REID
Everton

1986 - GARY LINEKER
Everton

1987 - CLIVE ALLEN
Tottenham Hostpur

1988 - JOHN BARNES
Liverpool

1989 - MARK HUGHES
Manchester United

1990 - DAVID PLATT
Aston Villa

1991 - MARK HUGHES
Manchester United

1992 - GARY PALLISTER
Manchester United

1993 - PAUL MCGRATH
Aston Villa

1994 - ERIC CANTONA
Manchester United

1995 - ALAN SHEARER
Blackburn Rovers

1996 - LES FERDINAND
Newcastle United

Gary Linekar, Everton

Mark Hughes,
Manchester United

1997 - ALAN SHEARER
Newcastle United

1998 - DENNIS BERGKAMP
Arsenal

1999 - DAVID GINOLA
Tottenham Hotspur

2000 - ROY KEANE
Manchester United

2001 - TEDDY SHERINGHAM
Manchester United

2002 - RUUD VAN NISTELROOY
Manchester United

2003 - THIERRY HENRY
Arsenal

2004 - THIERRY HENRY
Arsenal

2005 - JOHN TERRY
Chelsea

2006 - STEVEN GERRARD
Liverpool

2007 - CRISTIANO RONALDO
Manchester United

2008 - CRISTIANO RONALDO
Manchester United

2009 - RYAN GIGGS
Manchester United

2010 - WAYNE ROONEY
Manchester United

2011 - GARETH BALE
Tottenham Hotspur

2012 - ROBIN VAN PERSIE
Arsenal

2013 - GARETH BALE
Tottenham Hotspur

2014 - LUIS SUAREZ
Liverpool

MULTIPLE WINNERS (player)

MARK HUGHES
2 wins: 1989, 1991

ALAN SHEARER
2 wins: 1995, 1997

THIERRY HENRY
2 wins: 2003, 2004

CRISTIANO RONALDO
2 wins: 2007, 2008

GARETH BALE
2 wins: 2011, 2013

MULTIPLE WINNERS (club)

1ST MANCHESTER UNITED
11 wins: 1989, 1991, 1992, 1994, 2000, 2001, 2002, 2006, 2008, 2009, 2010

2ND LIVERPOOL
6 wins: 1980, 1983, 1984, 1988, 2006, 2014

3RD TOTTENHAM HOTSPUR
5 wins: 1976, 1987, 1999, 2011, 2013

ARSENAL
5 wins: 1979, 1998, 2003, 2004, 2012

5TH ASTON VILLA
3 wins: 1977, 1990, 1993

6TH EVERTON
2 wins: 1985, 1986

NEWCASTLE UNITED
2 wins: 1996, 1997

YOUNG PLAYER OF THE YEAR

1974 - KEVIN BEATTIE
Ipswich Town

1975 - MERVYN DAY
West Ham United

1976 - PETER BARNES
Manchester City

1977 - ANDY GRAY
Aston Villa

1978 - TONY WOODCOCK
Nottingham Forest

1979 - CYRILLE REGIS
West Bromwich Albion

1980 - GLENN HODDLE
Tottenham Hotspur

1981 - GARY SHAW
Aston Villa

1982 - STEVE MORAN
Southampton

1983 - IAN RUSH
Liverpool

1984 - PAUL WALSH
Luton Town

1985 - MARK HUGHES
Manchester United

1986 - TONY COTTEE
West Ham United

1987 - TONY ADAMS
Arsenal

1988 - PAUL GASCOIGNE
Newcastle United

1989 - PAUL MERSON
Arsenal

1990 - MATT LE TISSIER
Southampton

1991 - LEE SHARPE
Manchester United

1992 - RYAN GIGGS
Manchester United

1993 - RYAN GIGGS
Manchester United

1994 - ANDY COLE
Newcastle United

1995 - ROBBIE FOWLER
Liverpool

1996 - ROBBIE FOWLER
Liverpool

Paul Gascoigne,
Newcastle United

Ryan Giggs,
Manchester United

1997 - DAVID BECKHAM
Manchester United

1998 - MICHAEL OWEN
Liverpool

1999 - NICOLAS ANELKA
Arsenal

2000 - HARRY KEWELL
Leeds United

2001 - STEVEN GERRARD
Liverpool

2002 - CRAIG BELLAMY
Newcastle United

2003 - JERMAINE JENAS
Newcastle United

2004 - SCOTT PARKER
Charlton Athletic/Chelsea

2005 - WAYNE ROONEY
Manchester United

2006 - WAYNE ROONEY
Manchester United

2007 - CRISTIANO RONALDO
Manchester United

2008 - CESC FABREGAS
Arsenal

2009 - ASHLEY YOUNG
Aston Villa

2010 - JAMES MILNER
Aston Villa

2011 - JACK WILSHERE
Arsenal

2012 - KYLE WALKER
Tottenham Hotspur

2013 - GARETH BALE
Tottenham Hotspur

2014 - EDEN HAZARD
Chelsea

MULTIPLE WINNERS *(player)*

RYAN GIGGS
2 wins: 1992, 1993

ROBBIE FOWLER
2 wins: 1995, 1996

WAYNE ROONEY
2 wins: 2005, 2006

MULTIPLE WINNERS *(club)*

1ST MANCHESTER UNITED
8 wins: 1985, 1991, 1992, 1993, 1997, 2005, 2006, 2007

2ND ARSENAL
5 wins: 1987, 1989, 1999, 2008, 2011,

LIVERPOOL
5 wins: 1983, 1995, 1996, 1998, 2001

4TH ASTON VILLA
4 wins: 1977, 1981, 2009, 2010

NEWCASTLE UNITED
4 wins: 1988, 1994, 2002, 2003

6TH TOTTENHAM HOTSPUR
3 wins: 1980, 2012, 2013

7TH WEST HAM UNITED
2 wins: 1975, 1986

SOUTHAMPTON
2 wins: 1982, 1990

TEAMS OF THE YEAR

1974

GK - Pat Jennings, Tottenham Hotspur
DF - Paul Madeley, Leeds United
DF - Roy McFarland, Derby County
DF - Norman Hunter, Leeds United
DF - Colin Todd, Derby County
MF - Billy Bremner, Leeds United
MF - Tony Currie, Sheffield United
MF - Johnny Giles, Leeds United
FW - Mick Channon, Southampton
FW - Malcolm Macdonald, Newcastle United
FW - Allan Clarke, Leeds United

1975

GK - Peter Shilton, Stoke City
DF - Paul Madeley, Leeds United
DF - Gordon McQueen, Leeds United
DF - Kevin Beattie, Ipswich Town
DF - Colin Todd, Derby County
MF - Billy Bonds, West Ham United
MF - Colin Bell, Manchester City
MF - Alan Hudson, Stoke City
FW - Duncan McKenzie, Leeds United
FW - Bob Latchford, Everton
FW - Leighton James, Burnley

1976

GK - Pat Jennings, Tottenham Hotspur
DF - Paul Madeley, Leeds United
DF - Roy McFarland, Derby County
DF - Kevin Beattie, Ipswich Town
DF - Colin Todd, Derby County
MF - Kevin Keegan, Liverpool
MF - Don Masson, QPR
MF - Alan Hudson, Stoke City
FW - Duncan McKenzie, Leeds United
FW - John Toshack, Liverpool
FW - Dennis Tueart, Manchester City

1977

GK - Ray Clemence, Liverpool
DF - John Gidman, Aston Villa
DF - Roy McFarland, Derby County
DF - Kevin Beattie, Ipswich Town
DF - Mick Mills, Ipswich Town
MF - Kevin Keegan, Liverpool
MF - Brian Talbot, Ipswich Town
MF - Trevor Brooking, West Ham United
FW - Trevor Francis, Birmingham City
FW - Andy Gray, Aston Villa
FW - Dennis Tueart, Manchester City

1978

GK - Peter Shilton, Nottingham Forest
DF - John Gidman, Aston Villa
DF - Gordon McQueen, Leeds United
DF - Martin Buchan, Manchester United
DF - Derek Statham, West Bromwich Albion
MF - Steve Coppell, Manchester United
MF - Liam Brady, Arsenal
MF - Trevor Brooking, West Ham United
FW - Trevor Francis, Birmingham City
FW - Joe Jordan, Manchester United
FW - John Robertson, Nottingham Forest

Peter Shilton,
Stoke City

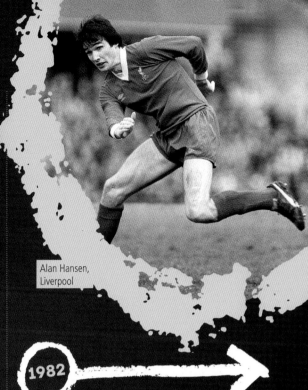

Alan Hansen,
Liverpool

1979

GK - Peter Shilton, Nottingham Forest
DF - Viv Anderson, Nottingham Forest
DF - David O'Leary, Arsenal
DF - Dave Watson, Manchester City
DF - Derek Statham, West Bromwich Albion
MF - Tony Currie, Leeds United
MF - Liam Brady, Arsenal
MF - Osvaldo Ardiles, Tottenham Hotspur
FW - Cyrille Regis, West Bromwich Albion
FW - Kenny Dalglish, Liverpool
FW - Laurie Cunningham, West Bromwich Albion

1980

GK - Peter Shilton, Nottingham Forest
DF - Viv Anderson, Nottingham Forest
DF - David O'Leary, Arsenal
DF - Dave Watson, Southampton
DF - Kenny Sansom, Crystal Palace
MF - Terry McDermott, Liverpool
MF - Liam Brady, Arsenal
MF - Glenn Hoddle, Tottenham Hotspur
FW - David Johnson, Liverpool
FW - Kenny Dalglish, Liverpool
FW - Garry Birtles, Nottingham Forest

1982

GK - Peter Shilton, Nottingham Forest
DF - Kenny Swain, Aston Villa
DF - David O'Leary, Arsenal
DF - Alan Hansen, Liverpool
DF - Kenny Sansom, Arsenal
MF - Glenn Hoddle, Tottenham Hotspur
MF - Bryan Robson, Manchester United
MF - Graeme Souness, Liverpool
FW - Trevor Francis, Manchester City
FW - Kevin Keegan, Liverpool
FW - Cyrille Regis, West Bromwich Albion

1981

GK - Peter Shilton, Nottingham Forest
DF - Kenny Swain, Aston Villa
DF - Russell Osman, Ipswich Town
DF - Allan Evans, Aston Villa
DF - Kenny Sansom, Arsenal
MF - Frans Thijssen, Ipswich Town
MF - John Wark, Ipswich Town
MF - Graeme Souness, Liverpool
FW - Paul Mariner, Ipswich Town
FW - Kenny Dalglish, Liverpool
FW - Gary Shaw, Aston Villa

1983

GK - Peter Shilton, Southampton
DF - Dennis Thomas, Coventry City
DF - Mark Lawrenson, Liverpool
DF - Alan Hansen, Liverpool
DF - Kenny Sansom, Arsenal
MF - Sammy Lee, Liverpool
MF - Bryan Robson, Manchester United
MF - Graeme Souness, Liverpool
FW - Ian Rush, Liverpool
FW - Kenny Dalglish, Liverpool
FW - Steve Coppell, Manchester United

TEAMS OF THE YEAR

1984

GK - Peter Shilton, Southampton
DF - Mike Duxberry, Manchester United
DF - Mark Lawrenson, Liverpool
DF - Alan Hansen, Liverpool
DF - Kenny Sansom, Arsenal
MF - Glenn Hoddle, Tottenham Hotspur
MF - Bryan Robson, Manchester United
MF - Graeme Souness, Liverpool
FW - Ian Rush, Liverpool
FW - Kenny Dalglish, Liverpool
FW - Frank Stapleton, Manchester United

1985

GK - Peter Shilton, Southampton
DF - Gary Stevens, Everton
DF - Mark Lawrenson, Liverpool
DF - Kevin Ratcliffe, Everton
DF - Kenny Sansom, Arsenal
MF - Peter Reid, Everton
MF - Bryan Robson, Manchester United
MF - Kevin Sheedy, Everton
FW - Ian Rush, Liverpool
FW - Chris Waddle, Newcastle United
FW - Kerry Dixon, Chelsea

1986

GK - Peter Shilton, Southampton
DF - Gary Stevens, Everton
DF - Mark Lawrenson, Liverpool
DF - Paul McGrath, Manchester United
DF - Kenny Sansom, Arsenal
MF - Glenn Hoddle, Tottenham Hotspur
MF - Bryan Robson, Manchester United
MF - Stewart Robson, Arsenal
FW - Gary Linekar, Everton
FW - Mark Hughes, Manchester United
FW - Paul Walsh, Liverpool

1987

GK - Neville Southall, Everton
DF - Viv Anderson, Arsenal
DF - Alan Hansen, Liverpool
DF - Tony Adams, Arsenal
DF - Kenny Sansom, Arsenal
MF - Glenn Hoddle, Tottenham Hotspur
MF - David Rocastle, Arsenal
MF - Kevin Sheedy, Everton
FW - Ian Rush, Liverpool
FW - Clive Allen, Tottenham Hotspur
FW - Peter Beardsley, Newcastle United

1988

GK - Neville Southall, Everton
DF - Gary Stevens, Everton
DF - Alan Hansen, Liverpool
DF - Gary Gillespie, Liverpool
DF - Stuart Pearce, Nottingham Forest
MF - Steve McMahon, Liverpool
MF - Peter Reid, Everton
MF - Paul Gascoigne, Newcastle United
MF - John Barnes, Liverpool
FW - Graeme Sharp, Everton
FW - Peter Beardsley, Liverpool

Kenny Dalglish, Liverpool

1989

GK - Neville Southall, Everton
DF - Steve Nicol, Liverpool
DF - Des Walker, Nottingham Forest
DF - Paul Parker, QPR
DF - Stuart Pearce, Nottingham Forest
MF - David Rocastle, Arsenal
MF - Bryan Robson, Manchester United
MF - Andy Townsend, Norwich City
MF - Chris Waddle, Tottenham Hotspur
FW - Mark Hughes, Manchester United
FW - Alan Smith, Arsenal

Stuart Pearce,
Nottingham Forest

1990

GK - Neville Southall, Everton
DF - Lee Dixon, Arsenal
DF - Des Walker, Nottingham Forest
DF - Alan Hansen, Liverpool
DF - Stuart Pearce, Nottingham Forest
MF - David Platt, Aston Villa
MF - Steve Hodge, Nottingham Forest
MF - Steve McMahon, Liverpool
MF - John Barnes, Liverpool
FW - Peter Beardsley, Liverpool
FW - Gary Lineker, Tottenham Hotspur

1992

GK - Tony Coton, Manchester City
DF - Rob Jones, Liverpool
DF - Gary Pallister, Manchester United
DF - Des Walker, Nottingham Forest
DF - Stuart Pearce, Nottingham Forest
MF - Ray Houghton, Liverpool
MF - Gary McAllister, Leeds United
MF - Andy Townsend, Chelsea
FW - Gary Lineker, Tottenham Hotspur
FW - Mark Hughes, Manchester United
FW - Alan Shearer, Southampton

1991

GK - David Seaman, Arsenal
DF - Lee Dixon, Arsenal
DF - Des Walker, Nottingham Forest
DF - Mark Wright, Derby County
DF - Stuart Pearce, Nottingham Forest
MF - Gordon Strachan, Leeds United
MF - Paul Gascoigne, Tottenham Hotspur
MF - Andy Townsend, Chelsea
MF - John Barnes, Liverpool
FW - Mark Hughes, Manchester United
FW - Ian Rush, Liverpool

1993

GK - Peter Schmeichel, Manchester United
DF - David Bardsley, QPR
DF - Paul McGrath, Aston Villa
DF - Gary Pallister, Manchester United
DF - Tony Dorigo, Leeds United
MF - Roy Keane, Nottingham Forest
MF - Gary Speed, Leeds United
MF - Paul Ince, Manchester United
MF - Ryan Giggs, Manchester United
FW - Ian Wright, Arsenal
FW - Alan Shearer, Blackburn Rovers

TEAMS OF THE YEAR

1994

GK - Tim Flowers, Blackburn Rovers
DF - Gary Kelly, Leeds United
DF - Gary Pallister, Manchester United
DF - Tony Adams, Arsenal
DF - Denis Irwin, Manchester United
MF - David Batty, Blackburn Rovers
MF - Gary McAllister, Leeds United
MF - Paul Ince, Manchester United
FW - Peter Beardsley, Newcastle United
FW - Eric Cantona, Manchester United
FW - Alan Shearer, Blackburn Rovers

1995

GK - Tim Flowers, Blackburn Rovers
DF - Rob Jones, Liverpool
DF - Gary Pallister, Manchester United
DF - Colin Hendry, Blackburn Rovers
DF - Graeme Le Saux, Blackburn Rovers
MF - Tim Sherwood, Blackburn Rovers
MF - Matthew Le Tissier, Southampton
MF - Paul Ince, Manchester United
FW - Jurgen Klinsmann, Tottenham Hotspur
FW - Chris Sutton, Blackburn Rovers
FW - Alan Shearer, Blackburn Rovers

1996

GK - David James, Liverpool
DF - Gary Neville, Manchester United
DF - Tony Adams, Arsenal
DF - Ugo Ehiogu, Aston Villa
DF - Alan Wright, Aston Villa
MF - Steve Stone, Nottingham Forest
MF - Rob Lee, Newcastle United
MF - Ruud Gullit, Chelsea
MF - David Ginola, Newcastle United
FW - Les Ferdinand, Newcastle United
FW - Alan Shearer, Blackburn Rovers

1997

GK - David Seaman, Arsenal
DF - Gary Neville, Manchester United
DF - Tony Adams, Arsenal
DF - Mark Wright, Liverpool
DF - Stig Inge Bjornebye, Liverpool
MF - David Beckham, Manchester United
MF - Roy Keane, Manchester United
MF - David Batty, Newcastle United
MF - Steve McManaman, Liverpool
FW - Ian Wright, Arsenal
FW - Alan Shearer, Newcastle United

1998

GK - Nigel Martyn, Leeds United
DF - Gary Neville, Manchester United
DF - Gary Pallister, Manchester United
DF - Colin Hendry, Blackburn Rovers
DF - Graeme Le Saux, Chelsea
MF - David Beckham, Manchester United
MF - Nicky Butt, Manchester United
MF - David Batty, Newcastle United
MF - Ryan Giggs, Manchester United
FW - Dennis Bergkamp, Arsenal
FW - Michael Owen, Liverpool

Graeme Le Saux,
Blackburn Rovers

1999

GK - Nigel Martyn, Leeds United
DF - Gary Neville, Manchester United
DF - Sol Campbell, Tottenham Hotspur
DF - Jaap Stam, Manchester United
DF - Denis Irwin, Manchester United
MF - David Beckham, Manchester United
MF - Emmanuel Petit, Arsenal
MF - Patrick Vieira, Arsenal
MF - David Ginola, Tottenham Hotspur
FW - Dwight Yorke, Manchester United
FW - Nicolas Anelka, Arsenal

Robert Pires,
Arsenal

2000

GK - Nigel Martyn, Leeds United
DF - Gary Kelly, Leeds United
DF - Jaap Stam, Manchester United
DF - Sami Hyypia, Liverpool
DF - Ian Harte, Leeds United
MF - David Beckham, Manchester United
MF - Roy Keane, Manchester United
MF - Patrick Vieira, Arsenal
MF - Harry Kewell, Leeds United
FW - Andrew Cole, Manchester United
FW - Kevin Phillips, Sunderland

2002

GK - Shay Given, Newcastle United
DF - Steve Finnan, Fulham
DF - Rio Ferdinand, Leeds United
DF - Sami Hyypia, Liverpool
DF - Wayne Bridge, Southampton
MF - Robert Pires, Arsenal
MF - Roy Keane, Manchester United
MF - Patrick Vieira, Arsenal
MF - Ryan Giggs, Manchester United
FW - Ruud van Nistelrooy, Manchester United
FW - Thierry Henry, Arsenal

2001

GK - Fabien Barthez, Manchester United
DF - Stephen Carr, Tottenham Hotspur
DF - Jaap Stam, Manchester United
DF - Wes Brown, Manchester United
DF - Sylvinho, Arsenal
MF - Steven Gerrard, Liverpool
MF - Roy Keane, Manchester United
MF - Patrick Vieira, Arsenal
MF - Ryan Giggs, Manchester United
FW - Teddy Sheringham, Manchester United
FW - Thierry Henry, Arsenal

2003

GK - Brad Friedel, Blackburn Rovers
DF - Stephen Carr, Tottenham Hotspur
DF - Sol Campbell, Arsenal
DF - William Gallas, Chelsea
DF - Ashley Cole, Arsenal
MF - Robert Pires, Arsenal
MF - Paul Scholes, Manchester United
MF - Patrick Vieira, Arsenal
MF - Kieron Dyer, Newcastle United
FW - Alan Shearer, Newcastle United
FW - Thierry Henry, Arsenal

TEAMS OF THE YEAR

2004

GK - Tim Howard, Manchester United
DF - Lauren, Arsenal
DF - Sol Campbell, Arsenal
DF - John Terry, Chelsea
DF - Ashley Cole, Arsenal
MF - Steven Gerrard, Liverpool
MF - Frank Lampard, Chelsea
MF - Patrick Vieira, Arsenal
MF - Robert Pires, Arsenal
FW - Ruud van Nistelrooy, Manchester United
FW - Thierry Henry, Arsenal

2005

GK - Petr Cech, Chelsea
DF - Gary Neville, Manchester United
DF - Rio Ferdinand, Manchester United
DF - John Terry, Chelsea
DF - Ashley Cole, Arsenal
MF - Steven Gerrard, Liverpool
MF - Frank Lampard, Chelsea
MF - Shaun Wright-Phillips, Manchester City
MF - Arjen Robben, Chelsea
FW - Andrew Johnson, Crystal Palace
FW - Thierry Henry, Arsenal

2006

GK - Shay Given, Newcastle United
DF - Pascal Chimbonda, Wigan Athletic
DF - Jamie Carragher, Liverpool
DF - John Terry, Chelsea
DF - William Gallas, Chelsea
MF - Steven Gerrard, Liverpool
MF - Frank Lampard, Chelsea
MF - Cristiano Ronaldo, Manchester United
MF - Joe Cole, Chelsea
FW - Wayne Rooney, Manchester United
FW - Thierry Henry, Arsenal

2007

GK - Edwin van der Sar, Manchester United
DF - Gary Neville, Manchester United
DF - Rio Ferdinand, Manchester United
DF - Nemanja Vidic, Manchester United
DF - Patrice Evra, Manchester United
MF - Steven Gerrard, Liverpool
MF - Paul Scholes, Manchester United
MF - Cristiano Ronaldo, Manchester United
MF - Ryan Giggs, Manchester United
FW - Didier Drogba, Chelsea
FW - Dimitar Berbatov, Tottenham Hotspur

2008

GK - David James, Portsmouth
DF - Bacary Sagna, Arsenal
DF - Rio Ferdinand, Manchester United
DF - Nemanja Vidic, Manchester United
DF - Gael Clichy, Arsenal
MF - Steven Gerrard, Liverpool
MF - Cesc Fabregas, Arsenal
MF - Cristiano Ronaldo, Manchester United
MF - Ashley Young, Aston Villa
FW - Emmanuel Adebayor, Arsenal
FW - Fernando Torres, Liverpool

Frank Lampard, Chelsea

2009

GK - Edwin van der Sar, Manchester United
DF - Glen Johnson, Portsmouth
DF - Rio Ferdinand, Manchester United
DF - Nemanja Vidic, Manchester United
DF - Patrice Evra, Manchester United
MF - Steven Gerrard, Liverpool
MF - Ryan Giggs, Manchester United
MF - Cristiano Ronaldo, Manchester United
MF - Ashley Young, Aston Villa
FW - Nicolas Anelka, Chelsea
FW - Fernando Torres, Liverpool

Fabricio Coloccini,
Newcastle United

2010

GK - Joe Hart, Birmingham City
DF - Branislav Ivanovic, Chelsea
DF - Thomas Vermaelen, Arsenal
DF - Richard Dunne, Aston Villa
DF - Patrice Evra, Manchester United
MF - Antonio Valencia, Manchester United
MF - Cesc Fabregas, Arsenal
MF - Darren Fletcher, Manchester United
MF - James Milner, Aston Villa
FW - Wayne Rooney, Manchester United
FW - Didier Drogba, Chelsea

2012

GK - Joe Hart, Manchester City
DF - Kyle Walker, Tottenham Hotspur
DF - Fabricio Coloccini, Newcastle United
DF - Vincent Kompany, Manchester City
DF - Leighton Baines, Everton
MF - David Silva, Manchester City
MF - Yaya Toure, Manchester City
MF - Scott Parker, Tottenham Hotspur
MF - Gareth Bale, Tottenham Hotspur
FW - Robin van Persie, Arsenal
FW - Wayne Rooney, Manchester United

2011

GK - Edwin van der Sar, Manchester United
DF - Bacary Sagna, Arsenal
DF - Nemanja Vidic, Manchester United
DF - Vincent Kompany, Manchester City
DF - Ashley Cole, Chelsea
MF - Nani, Manchester United
MF - Samir Nasri, Arsenal
MF - Jack Wilshere, Arsenal
MF - Gareth Bale, Tottenham Hotspur
FW - Carlos Tevez, Manchester City
FW - Dimitar Berbatov, Manchester United

2013

GK - David De Gea, Manchester United
DF - Pablo Zabaleta, Manchester City
DF - Rio Ferdinand, Manchester United
DF - Jan Vertonghen, Tottenham Hotspur
DF - Leighton Baines, Everton
MF - Michael Carrick, Manchester United
MF - Juan Mata, Chelsea
MF - Gareth Bale, Tottenham Hotspur
MF - Eden Hazard, Chelsea
FW - Robin van Persie, Manchester United
FW - Luis Suarez, Liverpool

2014

GOALKEEPER

PETR CECH, Chelsea
The Czech stopper started his second spell under Jose Mourinho like he left the first one - keeping clean sheets. The 32-year-old had 16 shout-outs during the campaign - the most in the league. The former Rennes star was also voted the best keeper to have ever played in the Premier League by fans in January.
PFA appearances: 2

DEFENDERS

SEAMUS COLEMAN, Everton
Has developed once again this year into one of Europe's best full-backs. Solid in defence and great going forward, the Republic of Ireland international runs all day for the Toffees. The Merseyside club conceded just 39 goals in Coleman's 36 league appearances which also saw the former Sligo Rovers man notch six Premier League goals.
PFA appearances: 1

VINCENT KOMPANY, Manchester City
The City skipper was selected for the third time in four years after another stellar campaign at the heart of the Citizens' defence. Despite injuries reducing his appearances to just 28, the Belgium skipper has seen just 30 goals go past him during those games as he lead by example once more to help the club clinch their second title in three years.
PFA appearances: 3

GARY CAHILL, Chelsea
The England defender was included for the first time after yet another year of consistency. His performances played a major part in the West London side having the best defensive record in the league, conceding just 26 times, as they challenged for a fourth Premier League title. The Blues conceded just 19 goals in the 31 games the ex-Bolton man was involved in.
PFA appearances: 1

LUKE SHAW, Southampton
After impressing in the last few months of the 2012-13 season, the talented left-back was one of the stars of this campaign. At just 18 years of age, the defender showed he has a massive future ahead of him with an array of top class performances which helped the club finished eighth and earned him an England debut and spot in the World Cup squad.
PFA appearances: 1

MIDFIELDERS

STEVEN GERRARD, Liverpool
The Liverpool captain was selected for an eighth time after yet another brilliant season for the Reds. Despite playing in a deeper role, the England captain scored 13 times in 34 appearances, including two penalties in the 3-0 win at Manchester United as the Merseyside club came agonisingly close to winning their first Premier League title.
PFA appearances: 8

Vincent Kompany, Manchester City

YAYA TOURE, Manchester City

The Ivorian was named in the side for the second time in three years after helping City win back the title. The powerful midfielder had his most prolific season to date as he scored 19 league goals in 35 matches including a number of stunning free-kicks. He also notched up seven assists and played 27 key passes throughout the campaign.
PFA appearances: 2

ADAM LALLANA, Southampton

The league's most improved player in the 2013-14 season, Lallana really showed that he is a top Premier League star. The playmaker added strength, speed and the ability to dominate a top-class match to the skill he'd always possessed. His nine goals, five assists and constant eye-catching performances saw him make his England debut and become a regular in the squad.
PFA appearances: 3 (2 in the Football League)

EDEN HAZARD, Chelsea

The Belgian's dazzling performances on the wing saw the talented youngster selected by his peers for the second time in his second year in England. His 14 goals - including a hat-trick against Newcastle United - and seven assists in 35 Premier League games bettered his first year at Stamford Bridge, earning him the PFA Young Player of the Year award.
PFA appearances: 2

STRIKERS →

DANIEL STURRIDGE, Liverpool

The England striker picked up where he left off the previous season by scoring in his first four Premier League games. The ex-Chelsea man hit the back of the net 21 times in 29 league appearances and clocked up seven assists. He was the highest scoring Englishman in the league and bettered his previous best in a domestic season by 10 goals.
PFA appearances: 1

PFA STRIKER →

LUIS SUAREZ,
Liverpool player

The South American superstar was the standout player of the season. Despite missing the first five games, the Reds' number 7 returned with a bang by scoring 31 times in 33 games. This made him just the seventh player to reach the 30 mark in a season that saw him win the division's Golden Boot and PFA Player of the Year award.
PFA appearances: 2

PREMIER LEAGUE PFA ALL TIME APPEARANCE MAKERS XI

GOALKEEPER

NIGEL MARTYN

Clubs when nominated: Leeds United
PFA Appearances: 3 ('98.'99,'00)
Premier League seasons: 11
Premier League appearances: 371
Premier League clean sheets: 138

*Edwin van der Sar has also appeared three times but kept less clean sheets than Martyn.

Nemanja Vidic,
Manchester United

DEFENDERS

ASHLEY COLE

Clubs when nominated: Arsenal, Chelsea
PFA Appearances: 4 ('03.'04,'05,'11)
Premier League seasons: 15
Premier League appearances: 385
Premier League goals: 15

NEMANJA VIDIC

Clubs when nominated: Manchester United
PFA Appearances: 4 ('07.'08,'09,'11)
Premier League seasons: 9
Premier League appearances: 211
Premier League goals: 15

RIO FERDINAND

Clubs when nominated: Leeds United, Manchester United
PFA Appearances: 6 ('02.'05,'07,'08,'09,'13)
Premier League seasons: 19
Premier League appearances: 493
Premier League goals: 11

GARY NEVILLE

Clubs when nominated: Manchester United
PFA Appearances: 6 ('96,'97,'98,'99,'05,'07)
Premier League seasons: 17
Premier League appearances: 400
Premier League goals: 5

MIDFIELDERS

ROY KEANE

Clubs when nominated: Nottingham Forest, Manchester United
PFA Appearances: 5 ('93,'97,'00,'01,'02)
Premier League seasons: 14
Premier League appearances: 366
Premier League goals: 39

Ashley Cole,
Chelsea

PATRICK VIEIRA

Clubs when nominated: Arsenal
PFA Appearances: 6 ('99,'00,'01,'02,'03,'04)
Premier League seasons: 11
Premier League appearances: 307
Premier League goals: 33

STEVEN GERRARD

Clubs when nominated: Liverpool
PFA Appearances: 8 ('01,'04,'05,'06,'07,'08,'09,'14)
Premier League seasons: 16
Premier League appearances: 475
Premier League goals: 111

RYAN GIGGS

Clubs when nominated: Manchester United
PFA Appearances: 6 ('93,'98,'01,'02,'07,'09)
Premier League seasons: 22
Premier League appearances: 632
Premier League goals: 109

STRIKERS

ALAN SHEARER

Clubs when nominated: Blackburn Rovers, Newcastle United
PFA Appearances: 6 ('93,'94,'95,'96,'97,'03)
Premier League seasons: 14
Premier League appearances: 441
Premier League goals: 260

THIERRY HENRY

Clubs when nominated: Arsenal
PFA Appearances: 6 ('01,'02,'03,'05,'05,'06)
Premier League seasons: 9
Premier League appearances: 258
Premier League goals: 176

Thierry Henry, Arsenal

FWA PLAYER of the Year

The Football Writers' Association (FWA) Footballer of the Year Award is was first handed out in 1948 to Blackpool winger Stanley Matthews, who is one of just eight players to have won the accolade on more than one occasion.

It was introduced following a suggestion made by Charles Buchan. The Plumstead born striker played for Sunderland and Arsenal, and was one of the FWA's founding members after turning to journalism following the end of his playing career.

The winner is voted for by members of the Football Writers' Association, made up of around 400 journalists based in England.

Liverpool's Luis Suarez was the latest recipient of the award.

1948 - **Stanley Matthews** (Blackpool)
1949 - **Johnny Carey** (Manchester United)
1950 - **Joe Mercer** (Arsenal)
1951 - **Harry Johnston** (Blackpool)
1952 - **Billy Wright** (Wolverhampton Wanderers)
1953 - **Nat Lofthouse** (Bolton Wanderers)
1954 - **Tom Finney** (Preston North End)
1955 - **Don Revie** (Manchester City)
1956 - **Bert Trautmann** (Manchester City)
1957 - **Tom Finney** (Preston North End)
1958 - **Danny Blanchflower**
    (Tottenham Hotspur)
1959 - **Syd Owen** (Luton Town)
1960 - **Bill Slater** (Wolverhampton Wanderers)
1961 - **Danny Blanchflower**
    (Tottenham Hotspur)
1962 - **Jimmy Adamson** (Burnley)
1963 - **Stanley Matthews** (Stoke City)
1964 - **Bobby Moore** (West Ham United)
1965 - **Bobby Collins** (Leeds United)
1966 - **Bobby Charlton** (Manchester United)
1967 - **Jack Charlton** (Leeds United)
1968 - **George Best** (Manchester United)
1969 - **Tony Brook** (Manchester City) and
    Dave Mackay (Derby County)
1970 - **Billy Bremner** (Leeds United)
1971 - **Frank McLintock** (Arsenal)
1972 - **Gordon Banks** (Stoke City)
1973 - **Pat Jennings** (Tottenham Hotspur)
1974 - **Ian Callaghan** (Liverpool)
1975 - **Alan Mullery** (Fulham)
1976 - **Kevin Keegan** (Liverpool)
1977 - **Emlyn Hughes** (Liverpool)
1978 - **Kenny Burns** (Nottingham Forest)
1979 - **Kenny Dalglish** (Liverpool)

1980 - **Terry McDermott** (Liverpool)
1981 - **Frans Thijssen** (Ipswich Town)
1982 - **Steve Perryman** (Tottenham Hotspur)
1983 - **Kenny Dalglish** (Liverpool)
1984 - **Ian Rush** (Liverpool)
1985 - **Neville Southall** (Everton)
1986 - **Gary Lineker** (Everton)
1987 - **Clive Allen** (Tottenham Hostpur)
1988 - **John Barnes** (Liverpool)
1989 - **Steve Nicol** (Liverpool)
1990 - **John Barnes** (Liverpool)
1991 - **Gordon Strachan** (Leeds United)
1992 - **Gary Lineker** (Tottenham Hotspur)
1993 - **Chris Waddle** (Sheffield Wednesday)
1994 - **Alan Shearer** (Blackburn Rovers)
1995 - **Jurgen Klinsmann** (Tottenham Hotspur)
1996 - **Eric Cantona** (Manchester United)
1997 - **Gianfranco Zola** (Chelsea)
1998 - **Dennis Bergkamp** (Arsenal)
1999 - **David Ginola** (Tottenham Hotspur)
2000 - **Roy Keane** (Manchester United)
2001 - **Teddy Sheringham** (Manchester United)
2002 - **Robert Pires** (Arsenal)
2003 - **Thierry Henry** (Arsenal)
2004 - **Thierry Henry** (Arsenal)
2005 - **Frank Lampard** (Chelsea)
2006 - **Thierry Henry** (Arsenal)
2007 - **Cristiano Ronaldo** (Manchester United)
2008 - **Cristiano Ronaldo** (Manchester United)
2009 - **Steven Gerrard** (Liverpool)
2010 - **Wayne Rooney** (Manchester United)
2011 - **Scott Parker** (West Ham United)
2012 - **Robin van Persie** (Arsenal)
2013 - **Gareth Bale** (Tottenham Hotspur)
2014 - **Luis Suarez** (Liverpool)

MULTIPLE WINNERS

Thierry Henry
3 wins: 2003, 2004, 2006

Cristiano Ronaldo
2 wins: 2007, 2008

Gary Lineker
2 wins: 1986, 1992

John Barnes
2 wins: 1988, 1990

Kenny Dalglish
2 wins: 1979, 1983

Danny Blanchflower
2 wins: 1958, 1961

Tom Finney
2 wins: 1954, 1957

Stanley Matthews
2 wins: 1948, 1963

WINNERS BY CLUB

Eric Cantona, Manchester United, 1996.

1st

Liverpool
11 wins: 1974, 1976, 1977, 1979, 1980, 1983, 1984, 1988, 1989, 1990, 2009

2nd

Manchester United
9 wins: 1949, 1966, 1968, 1996, 2000, 2001, 2007, 2008, 2010

Tottenham Hotspur
9 wins: 1958, 1961, 1973, 1982, 1987, 1992, 1995, 1999, 2013

4th
Arsenal
8 wins: 1950, 1971, 1998, 2002, 2003, 2004, 2006, 2012

5th
Leeds United
4 wins: 1965, 1967, 1970, 1991

6th
Manchester City
3 wins: 1955, 1956, 1969

Premier League
MANAGER
of the Season

The Premier League Manager of the Season award recognises the top flight's most impressive manager of each campaign.

The winner is picked by a panel assembled by the league's main sponsor.

There was not an award in the inaugural year of what is now seen as the most exciting division in the world as the Premier League didn't find a sponsor until their second season, coinciding with the introduction of the award.

Sir Alex Ferguson was the first recipient and has won the accolade an incredible 11 times in its 21-year history.

Crystal Palace's Tony Pulis is the latest boss to collect the gong.

1994 Alex Ferguson
Nationality: Scottish
Club: Manchester United
Achievement: Defending the title in the Premier League's second season by collecting 92 points.

1995 Kenny Dalglish
Nationality: Scottish
Club: Blackburn Rovers
Achievement: Surprising English football to win their first top flight title in 81 years.

1996 Alex Ferguson
Nationality: Scottish
Club: Manchester United
Achievement: Securing the Red Devils' third Premier League title in four seasons, clawing back a 12-point deficit on Newcastle United in the final couple of months.

1997 Alex Ferguson
Nationality: Scottish
Club: Manchester United
Achievement: Winning a fourth title in five years, again ahead of Newcastle United.

1998 Arsene Wenger
Nationality: French
Club: Arsenal
Achievement: Guiding The Gunners to the league and cup double for the first time in his first full season in charge.

1999 Alex Ferguson
Nationality: Scottish
Club: Manchester United
Achievement: Winning the club's 11th English league title and fifth Premier League trophy in seven seasons.

2000 Alex Ferguson
Nationality: Scottish
Club: Manchester United
Achievement: Successfully defending the league trophy, finishing 18 points ahead of runners-up Arsenal.

2001 George Burley
Nationality: Scottish
Club: Ipswich Town
Achievement: Finishing fifth a year after winning promotion to the Premier League for the first time.

2002 Arsene Wenger
Nationality: French
Club: Arsenal
Achievement: Winning The Gunners' second Premier League title in four years.

2003 Alex Ferguson
Nationality: Scottish
Club: Manchester United
Achievement: Collecting an eighth Premier League title, regaining the crown from Arsenal.

2004 Arsene Wenger
Nationality: French
Club: Arsenal
Achievement: Becoming just the second side, since Preston North End in 1880, to go a whole English league season unbeaten.

2005 Jose Mourinho
Nationality: Portuguese
Club: Chelsea
Achievement: Winning The Blues' first top flight title for 50 years with a record points total (95), most wins (29) and fewest goals conceded (15) in a Premier League season.

2006 Jose Mourinho
Nationality: Portuguese
Club: Chelsea
Achievement: Successfully defending the Premier League title.

2007 Alex Ferguson
Nationality: Scottish
Club: Manchester United
Achievement: Securing United's ninth Premier League title and first since 2003.

2008 Alex Ferguson
Nationality: Scottish
Club: Manchester United
Achievement: Winning his 10th Premier League title and United's 17th top flight crown.

2009 Alex Ferguson
Nationality: Scottish
Club: Manchester United
Achievement: lifting United's third successive Premier League trophy and 11th in 17 years.

2010 Harry Redknapp
Nationality: English
Club: Tottenham Hotspur
Achievement: Securing Champions League qualification for the first time in the club's history by achieving a fourth place finish.

2011 Alex Ferguson
Nationality: Scottish
Club: Manchester United
Achievement: Leading United to their 12th Premier League crown.

2012 Alan Pardew
Nationality: English
Club: Newcastle United
Achievement: Guiding Newcastle to fifth place in the Premier League - just four points off a Champions League place.

2013 Alex Ferguson
Nationality: Scottish
Club: Manchester United
Achievement: Winning his 13th Premier League crown with United.

2014 Tony Pulis
Nationality: Welsh
Club: Crystal Palace
Achievement: When Pulis took over at Selhurts Park in November, the Eagles were heading for relegation. But 11 wins and just five defeats from 26 games secured the South London side's top flight status.

Tony Pulis
2014

MULTIPLE WINNERS

1st

Alex Ferguson
Wins: 11 (1994, 1996, 1997, 1999, 2000, 2003, 2007, 2008, 2009, 2011, 2013)

2nd

Arsene Wenger
Wins: 3 (1998, 2002, 2004)

3rd

Jose Mourinho
Wins: 2 (2005, 2006)

WINNERS BY CLUB

1st

Manchester United
Wins: 11 - Alex Ferguson (11)

2nd

Arsenal
Wins: 3 - Arsene Wenger (3)

3rd

Chelsea
Wins: 2 - Jose Mourinho (2)

BY NATIONALITY

1st

Scotland
Wins: 13 - Alex Ferguson (11), Kenny Dalglish, George Burley

2nd

France
Wins: 3 - Arsene Wenger (3)

3rd

Portugal
Wins: 2 - Jose Mourinho (2)

4th

England
Wins: 2 - Alan Pardew, Harry Redknapp,

LMA MANAGER of the Year

The League Managers Association (LMA), which was established in 1992, is the trade union for Premier League, Football League and national team mangers in English football - just like the PFA is the players' trade union.

In 1994 the LMA started handing out their prestigious Manager of the Year Award. The winner is voted for by fellow bosses and, unlike the Premier League's equivalent, can come from any of England's top four divisions.

Joe Kinnear was the first winner after guiding Wimbledon to sixth place in the Premier League, while Brendan Rodgers of Liverpool is the latest recipient.

1994 Joe Kinnear
Nationality: Irish
Club: Wimbledon
League: Premier League
Achievement: Equalling thee Dons' highest ever league finish - sixth in 1987.

1995 Frank Clark
Nationality: English
Club: Nottingham Forest
League: Premier League
Achievement: Finishing third in the top flight - the highest a newly promoted club has achieved in Premier League history.

1996 Peter Reid
Nationality: English
Club: Sunderland
League: Division One
Achievement: Guiding the Black Cats to the Premier League for the first time by winning the Division 1 championship a year after saving the club from relegation.

1997 Danny Wilson
Nationality: Northern Irish
Club: Barnsley
League: Division One
Achievement: Securing promotion to the top tier of English football for the first time in the club's history.

1998 Dave Jones
Nationality: English
Club: Southampton
League: Premier League
Achievement: Taking Saints to a 12th place finish despite losing seven of the opening nine league matches and having not previously managed higher than the fourth division.

1999 Alex Ferguson
Nationality: Scottish
Club: Manchester United
League: Premier League
Achievement: Winning the Champions League, FA Cup and Premier League treble.

2000 Alan Curbishley
Nationality: English
Club: Charlton Athletic
League: Division One
Achievement: Taking the Addicks back to the Premier League at the first time of asking by winning the Division 1 title.

2001 George Burley
Nationality: Scottish
Club: Ipswich Town
League: Premier League
Achievement: Finishing fifth and qualifying for the UEFA Cup despite being a newly-promoted side.

2002 Arsene Wenger
Nationality: French **Club:** Arsenal
League: Premier League
Achievement: Winning his second Premier League and FA Cup double in four years.

2003 David Moyes
Nationality: Scottish **Club:** Everton
League: Premier League
Achievement: Guiding The Toffees to seventh place in his first season in charge.

2004 Arsene Wenger
Nationality: French **Club:** Arsenal
League: Premier League
Achievement: Becoming just the second side, since Preston North End in 1880, to go a whole English league season unbeaten.

2005 David Moyes
Nationality: Scottish
Club: Everton
League: Premier League
Achievement: Finishing fourth and qualifying for the Champions League despite being tipped for relegation.

2006 Steve Coppell
Nationality: English
Club: Reading
League: Championship
Achievement: Securing promotion to the Premier League for the first time by winning the Championship with a record 106 points.

2007 Steve Coppell
Nationality: English
Club: Reading
League: Premier League
Achievement: guiding Reading to eight place in their first Premier League season.

2008 Alex Ferguson
Nationality: Scottish
Club: Manchester United
League: Premier League
Achievement: Winning his second Champions League and 10th Premier League title.

2009 David Moyes
Nationality: Scottish
Club: Everton
League: Premier League
Achievement: FA Cup runners-up and a fifth placed finish in the Premier League.

2010 Roy Hodgson
Nationality: English **Club:** Fulham
League: Premier League
Achievement: Reaching the Europa League final and finishing safely in mid-table.

2011 Alex Ferguson
Nationality: Scottish
Club: Manchester United
League: Premier League
Achievement: Leading United to their 12th Premier League crown and the Champions League final.

2012 Alan Pardew
Nationality: English
Club: Newcastle United
League: Premier League
Achievement: Guiding Newcastle to fifth place in the Premier League.

2013 Alex Ferguson
Nationality: Scottish
Club: Manchester United
League: Premier League
Achievement: Winning his 13th Premier League crown and the club's 20th top flight title.

2014 Brendan Rodgers
Nationality: Northern Irish
Club: Liverpool
League: Premier League
Achievement: Guided Liverpool to a surprise second placed finish, finishing just two points behind champions Manchester City.

MULTIPLE WINNERS

1st

Alex Ferguson
Wins: 4 (1999, 2008, 2011, 2013)

2nd

David Moyes
Wins: 3 (2003, 2005, 2009)

3rd

Arsene Wenger
Wins: 2 (2002, 2004)

4th

Steve Coppell
Wins: 2 (2006, 2007)

WINNERS BY CLUB

1st

Manchester United
Wins: 4 - Alex Ferguson (4)

2nd

Everton
Wins: 3 - David Moyes (3)

3rd

Arsenal
Wins: 2 - Arsene Wenger (3)

4th

Reading
Wins: 2 - Steve Coppell (2)

BY NATIONALITY

1st

England
Wins: 8 - Steve Coppell (2), Alan Pardew, Roy Hodgson, Alan Curbishley, Dave Jones, Peter Reid, Frank Clark

Scotland
Wins: 8 - Alex Ferguson (4), David Moyes (3), George Burley

3rd

France
Wins: 2 - Arsene Wenger (2)

European GOLDEN Shoe

The European Golden Shoe, previously known as the European Golden Boot, is a trophy every attacker dreams of getting their hands on.

The award, first handed out in 1968 to Benfica and Portugal legend Eusebio, recognises the best goalscorer from across the European leagues in a season.

But this doesn't necessarily mean you have to notch the most league goals to land this prestigious prize. Since the 1996-97 season the Golden Shoe has been based on a points system, allowing players in the major leagues the chance to get in on the action.

The decision was made to change the format after players from the Georgian, Armenian and Welsh leagues claimed the prize in 1994, 1995 and 1996 respectively.

Here are the previous recipients of the European Golden Shoe.

1967-68
Eusebio
Club: Benfica
League: Portuguese Primeira Liga
Goals: 43

1968-69
Petar Zhekov
Club: CSKA Sofia
League: Bulgarian A PFG
Goals: 36

1969-70
Gerd Muller
Club: Bayern Munich
League: Bundesliga
Goals: 38

1970-71
Josip Skoblar
Club: Marseille
League: Ligue 1
Goals: 44

1971-72
Gerd Muller
Club: Bayern Munich
League: Bundesliga
Goals: 40

1972-73
Eusebio
Club: Benfica
League: Portuguese Primeira Liga
Goals: 40

1973-74
Hector Yazalde
Club: Sporting Lisbon
League: Portuguese Primeira Liga
Goals: 46

1974-75
Dudu Georgescu
Club: Dinamo Bucharest
League: Romanian Divizia A
Goals: 33

1975-76
Sotiris Kaiafas
Club: Omonia Nicosia
League: Cypriot First Division
Goals: 39

1976-77
Dudu Georgescu
Club: Dinamo Bucharest
League: Romanian Divizia A
Goals: 37

1977-78
Hans Krankl
Club: Rapid Vienna
League: Austrian Bundesliga
Goals: 41

1978-79
Kees Kist
Club: AZ Alkmaar
League: Dutch Eredivisie
Goals: 34

1979-80
Erwin Vandenbergh
Club: Lierse
League: Belgian League
Goals: 39

1980-81
Georgi Slavkov
Club: Botev Plovdiv
League: Bulgarian A PFG
Goals: 31

1981-82
Wim Kieft
Club: Ajax
League: Dutch Eredivisie
Goals: 32

1982-83
Fernando Gomes
Club: Porto
League: Portuguese Primeira Liga
Goals: 36

1983-84
Ian Rush
Club: Liverpool
League: English First Division
Goals: 32

1984-85
Fernando Gomes
Club: Porto
League: Portuguese Primeira Liga
Goals: 39

1985-86
Marco van Basten
Club: Ajax
League: Dutch Eredivisie
Goals: 37

1986-87
Rodion Camataru
Club: Dinamo Bucharest
League: Romanian Divizia A
Goals: 44

1987-88
Tanju Colak
Club: Galatasaray
League: Super Lig
Goals: 39

1988-89
Dorin Mateut
Club: Dinamo Bucharest
League: Romanian Divizia A
Goals: 43

1989-90
Hugo Sanchez & Hristo Stoichkov
Club: Real Madrid and CSKA Sofia
League: Spanish La Liga and Bulgarian A PFG
Goals: 38

1990-91
Darko Pancev
Club: Red Star
League: Yugoslav First League
Goals: 34

1991-92
Ally McCoist
Club: Rangers
League: Scottish Premier Division
Goals: 34

1992-93
Ally McCoist
Club: Rangers
League: Scottish Premier Division
Goals: 34

1993-94
David Taylor
Club: Porthmadog
League: League of Wales
Goals: 43

1994-95
Arsen Avetisyan
Club: Homenetmen
League: Armenian Premier League
Goals: 39

1995-96
Zviad Endeladze
Club: Margveti
League: Georgian Umaglesi Liga
Goals: 40

1996-97
Ronaldo
Club: Barcelona
League: Spanish La Liga
Goals: 34

1997-98
Nikos Machlas
Club: Vitesse
League: Dutch Eredivisie
Goals: 34

1998-99
Mario Jardel
Club: Porto
League: Portuguese Primeira Liga
Goals: 36

1999-00
Kevin Phillips
Club: Sunderland
League: English Premier League
Goals: 30

2000-01
Henrik Larsson
Club: Celtic
League: Scottish Premier League
Goals: 35

2001-02
Mario Jardel
Club: Sporting Lisbon
League: Portuguese Primeira Liga
Goals: 42

2002-03
Roy Makaay
Club: Deportivo La Coruna
League: Spanish La Liga
Goals: 29

2003-04
Thierry Henry
Club: Arsenal
League: English Premier League
Goals: 30

2004-05
Thierry Henry & Diego Forlan
Club: Arsenal and Villarreal
League: English Premier League and Spanish La Liga
Goals: 25

2005-06
Luca Toni
Club: Fiorentina
League: Italian Serie A
Goals: 31

2006-07
Francesco Totti
Club: Roma
League: Italian Serie A
Goals: 26

2007-08
Cristiano Ronaldo
Club: Manchester United
League: English Premier League
Goals: 31

2008-09
Diego Forlan
Club: Atletico Madrid
League: Spanish La Liga
Goals: 32

2009-10
Lionel Messi
Club: Barcelona
League: Spanish La Liga
Goals: 34

2010-11
Cristiano Ronaldo
Club: Real Madrid
League: Spanish La Liga
Goals: 40

2011-12
Lionel Messi
Club: Barcelona
League: Spanish La Liga
Goals: 50

2012-13
Lionel Messi
Club: Barcelona
League: Spanish La Liga
Goals: 46

2013-14
Luis Suarez & Cristiano Ronaldo
Clubs: Liverpool and Real Madrid
Leagues: English Premier League and Spanish La Liga
Goals: 31

2008

BIGGEST STADIUMS

20 ESTÁDIO DO MARACANÃ

Where: Rio de Janeiro, Brazil
Team: Flamengo and Fluminense
Capacity: 78,838
Opened: 1950

Originally built for the 1950 World Cup, the stadium incredibly held 199,854 spectators for the final against Uruguay. The venue currently hosts the home matches of Brazilian club teams Flamengo and Fluminense, but following the collapse of an upper stand in 1992 this original capacity was significantly reduced as the arena became all-seater. The stadium was partially rebuilt in 2013 in preparation for the Confederations Cup, the 2014 World Cup, where it will again host the final, and the 2016 Olympic and Paralympic Games.

19 STADE DES MARTYRS

Where: Kinshasa, DR Congo
Team: DR Congo national side, AS Vita club and DC Motema Pembe
Capacity: 80,000
Opened: 1994

Originally built by the Chinese when the Democratic Republic of Congo was known as Zaire, this stadium now hosts the international matches of the DR Congo national team, as well as two Congolese club sides - AS Vita Club and DC Motema Pembe. Its official capacity is 80,000, but it has often been suggested that up to 100,000 spectators have been present at some matches. In 2008 the venue was renovated by the government to meet international standards, as recommended by FIFA.

S tadiums are football's theatres. They are the places we go to watch the world's superstars perform on a weekly basis. Some cater for large numbers of people while others serve a smaller crowd. However, due to the demands for major tournament stadiums, club developments and changes in health and safety rules, the places the fans will proudly call their second home are changing all the time.

There are some amazing and historic stadiums such as the Allianz Arena in Munich, Manchester United's Old Trafford and Marseille's Stade Velodrome, but what are the biggest stadiums on the planet? Here's the top 20.

18 SHANGHAI STADIUM

Where: Shanghai, China
Team: Shanghai East Asia FC
Capacity: 80,000
Opened: 1997

Now the home of Shanghai East Asia FC, who were founded in 2005, the stadium was originally built for the 1997 National Games of the People's Republic of China. The arena also hosted a number of preliminary football matches during the 2008 Olympic Games. Following the end of the Games, Shanghai East Asia took up residency of the stadium to play their Chinese Super League home fixtures. One of the stadium's most prominent features is its saddle-shaped roof.

17 SAN SIRO

Where: Milan, Italy
Team: AC Milan and Internazionale
Capacity: 80,018
Opened: 1926

The oldest stadium in the top 20, the San Siro is currently home to two of the biggest football clubs in Italy and Europe - AC Milan and Internazionale. As well as those two sides, the Italian national team also play occasional international matches at the venue, while it has also hosted three European Cup finals. The stadium has undergone a number of renovations with one of the main refurbishments coming before the 1990 World Cup, when an extra tier was added to three sides of the structure as it became all-seater.

16 ESTADIO MONUMENTAL

Where: Lima, Peru
Team: Club Universitario de Deportes
Capacity: 80,093
Opened: 2000

The largest stadium in South America, this modern venue is home to one of the biggest club teams in Peru - Club Univesitario de Deportes - while it has also been known to host some of the Peru national side's international matches, including World Cup qualifiers. The stadium is divided into two main sections - the lower stands are for the general public and the upper stand consists of six floors of luxury boxes. Between 2000-07 the major Peruvian derby between Universitario and Alianza Lima was only played once in the stadium due to security concerns.

15 LUZHNIKI STADIUM

Where: Moscow, Russia
Team: Russia national side
Capacity: 81,000
Opened: 1956

Located in the Russian capital, this stadium is where the Russia national football team play their home international matches, while one of the country's biggest club sides - FC Spartak Moscow - were also based here before the opening of their new stadium in the summer of 2014. It is one of the few stadia to incorporate an artificial pitch because the grass isn't able to deal with the harsh winters. Despite that, it did host the 2008 Champions League final between Manchester United and Chelsea, and has been selected to host the 2018 World Cup final.

14 SANTIAGO BERNABEU

Where: Madrid, Spain
Team: Real Madrid
Capacity: 81,044
Opened: 1947

One of the oldest and most prestigious stadiums in this list, and home to one of the most famous football clubs in the world, it got its name in honour of former Real Madrid chairman Santiago Bernabéu Yeste. There are plans, which will include a retractable roof, to increase the capacity to 88,500 at a cost of around £330m. The venue has hosted four European Cup finals, a Champions League final, and the 1982 World Cup final, while the Spain national side have also hosted international matches at the venue.

13 SIGNAL IDUNA PARK

Where: Dortmund, Germany
Team: Borussia Dortmund
Capacity: 81,264
Opened: 1974

Also commonly referred to as the Westfalenstadion, this is the home of the German giants Borussia Dortmund and is one of the most famous stadiums in world football. One of the reasons for this is because of its South Bank terrace, which can hold over 24,000 standing spectators. Famous for the atmosphere it can create, it has been nicknamed the "Yellow Wall". The venue played host to six matches during the 2006 World Cup, and has undergone a number of expansions since it was built in 1974.

12 STADE DE FRANCE

Where: Paris, France
Team: France national side
Capacity: 81,338
Opened: 1998

When France were selected to host the 1998 World Cup, the country had no stadium that could seat more than 45,000 spectators, so the Stade de France was constructed on the outskirts of Paris, the French capital. The name of the venue was suggested by Michel Platini, and France went on to beat Brazil 3-1 in the final at the stadium on a special day for 'Les Bleus'. In the modern day, it is the home of the France national football team, as well as hosting the country's major domestic cup finals.

11 ANZ STADIUM

Where: Sydney, Australia
Team: Australia national side
Capacity: 83,500
Opened: 1999

Purpose built for the 2000 Olympic and Paralympic Games, the ANZ Stadium was originally created to seat 110,000 people, but in 2003 that was reduced following the removal of the south and north upper stands. As the largest capacity stadium in Australia that can be configured for rectangular field sports, it hosts a large number of matches for the Australia national team, while Manchester United beat the A-League All Stars in front of a record attendance for football at the venue in 2013.

10 AZADI STADIUM

Where: Tehran, Iran
Team: Iran national side,
Persepolis FC and Esteghlal FC
Capacity: 84,412
Opened: 1973

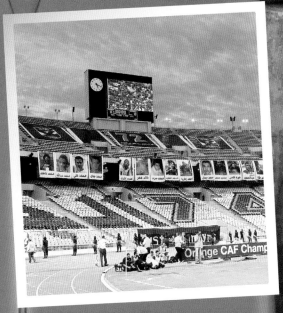

Self-owned by two of Iran's biggest
club sides - Persepolis FC and Esteghlal
FC - as well as hosting the matches of
the Iran national football team, the
Azadi Stadium was originally built for
the 1974 Asian Games. At that time it
was able to hold around 100,000
spectators, but the capacity was
reduced following a refurbishment
which was completed in 2003. The
record attendance at the striking venue
came in 1998 during a World Cup
qualifier against Australia when the
crowd swelled to over 128,000.

9 BORG EL ARAB STADIUM

Where: Alexandria, Egypt
Team: Egypt national side
Capacity: 86,000
Opened: 2007

Located near to where the Egyptian
coast meets the Mediterranean sea, the
Borg El Arab is another relatively new
stadium. The second largest stadium in
Africa, it has become one of the homes
of the Egypt national side, but due to its
running track, can also host the Olympic
Games. Only one of the stands is
covered by a roof, although the terrace
and first-class stands are protected by a
metal sunshade. One interesting
amenity the stadium holds is a
helicopter pad, which can hold up to
four aircraft.

8 GELORA BUNG KARNO STADIUM

Where: Jakarta, Indonesia
Team: Indonesia national side and Persija Jakarta
Capacity: 88,083
Opened: 1962

Located in the capital city of Indonesia, The Gelora Bung Karno Main Stadium is part of a sports complex that also includes venues such as swimming and tennis arenas. The venue was completed in 1962 just before it hosted the fourth Asian games. The stadium originally seated more than 120,000 people but this was reduced before the 2007 Asian Cup. It now plays host to the Indonesia national football team, as well as one of their biggest club sides - Persija Jakarta. Arsenal, Chelsea and Liverpool all appeared there as part of their 2013 pre-season tours.

7 WEMBLEY STADIUM

Where: London, England
Team: England national side
Capacity: 90,000
Opened: 2007

Built on the site of the old iconic Wembley Stadium, this is one of the newest venues in this list. The London ground is the second largest stadium in Europe and is the home of all of England's home international matches. As well as this, it also hosts a number of domestic cup finals - and in the case of the FA Cup - the semi-finals - as well as the play-off finals in each of the Football Leagues. Despite being so modern, Wembley has also already hosted the Champions League final twice - in 2011 and 2013.

6 FNB STADIUM

Where: Johannesburg, South Africa
Team: South Africa national side and Kaizer Chiefs
Capacity: 94,736
Opened: 1989

Known as Soccer City during the 2010 World Cup in South Africa, this stadium was the centrepiece for the tournament and where the final was held between Holland and Spain. The venue hosts the home matches of the South Africa national team, as well as one of the biggest club sides in the nation - Kaizer Chiefs. The stadium has also been nicknamed 'The Calabash', because of its similarity to the shape and appearance of an Afrian pot by the same name, following its pre-World Cup renovation in 2009.

5 CAMP NOU

Where: Barcelona, Spain
Team: FC Barcelona
Capacity: 99,786
Opened: 1957

Because of the success of the team that plays their home matches here - FC Barcelona - in recent years, the Camp Nou has become one of the most iconic stadiums in club football. It has been the home of the Catalan giants for nearly 60 years and at its highest point, reaches 48m above ground level. When it played host to the 1982 FIFA World Cup, the stadium had crowds that exceeded 120,000, and there are plans to increase the current capacity to 105,000 - a development that will cost around £500m and should be complete in 2021.

4 BUKIT JALIL NATIONAL STADIUM

Where: Kuala Lumpur, Malaysia
Team: Malaysia national side
Capacity: 100,200
Opened: 1998

Located just to the south of the capital of Malaysia - Kuala Lumpur - this stadium was originally built to host the 1998 Commonwealth Games. Following the end of the Games in September of that year, the venue then became the home of the Malaysia national team. The stadium has also played host to a number of English sides on their pre-season tours including Liverpool, Chelsea, Arsenal and Manchester United. The three-tiered structure is also able to host athletics because of the purpose it was originally constructed for.

3 ESTADIO AZTECA

Where: Mexico City, Mexico
Team: Mexico national side and Club América
Capacity: 105,064
Opened: 1966

Widely considered as one of the most iconic stadiums in world football, The Estadio Azteca is the home of the Mexico national side, as well as one of the country's biggest domestic teams - Club América. The name of the stadium pays tribute to the heritage of Mexico City, and the venue became the first to host two World Cup finals - in 1970 and 1986 - and was the stage in which Diego Maradona scored his famous 'Hand of God' goal against England. Again it is a multi-purpose venue and was one of the primary sites used in the 1968 Summer Olympic Games.

② SALT LAKE STADIUM

Where: Kolkata, India
Team: India national side, Mohun Bagan AC, East Bengal FC and Mohammedan SC
Capacity: 120,000
Opened: 1984

This stadium got its name as the town it is situated in - Bidhannagar - was built on a saltwater lake. It is a multi-purpose venue that is primarily used for football, hosting the matches of the India national side, as well as being the home of a number of domestic teams. The venue hosted Oliver Kahn's last ever match for Bayern Munich as they played Mohun Bagan in a friendly match in 2008. The capacity looks set to be reduced to 80,000 in time for the 2017 FIFA Under-17 World Cup.

① RUNGNADO MAY DAY STADIUM

Where: Pyongyang, North Korea
Team: North Korea national side
Capacity: 150,000
Opened: 1989

Regarded as the largest stadium in the world, the Rungnado May Day Stadium in North Korea is mainly used for football matches involving both the North Korea men's and women's national sides. Athletics can also be hosted at the venue, where the roof is made up of 16 arches arranged in a ring, which is said to resemble a magnolia blossom, while the roof structure reaches more than 60m above ground level. The multi-purpose structure is also well known for hosting celebrations of the nation of North Korea and their former leader Kim Il-sung.

TOP
TRANSF£RS

Transfers have always been a massive part of the beautiful game but they have become more prominent in the modern day due to the huge amounts of money players are being bought for. Since Italian striker Giuseppe Savoldi became the first £1 million pound player in 1975, fees have been constantly on the rise with the current record a staggering 86 times that amount. Here are the world's 10 biggest transfers.

1 Gareth Bale

From: Tottenham Hotspur To: Real Madrid

£86m

2

Cristiano Ronaldo

From: Manchester United
To: Real Madrid

£80m

3

Neymar Jr

From: Santos
To: Barcelona

£71m

4

Zlatan Ibrahmivoic

From: Inter Milan
To: Barcelona

£60m

5 Kaka

From: AC Milan
To: Real Madrid

£56m

6 Edinson Cavani

From: Napoli
To: Paris St-Germain

£55.6m

7 Radamel Falcao

From: Atletico Madrid
To: AS Monaco

£51m

8 Fernando Torres

From: Liverpool
To: Chelsea

£50m

9 Zinedine Zidane

From: Juventus
To: Real Madrid

£46.2m

10 Mesut Ozil

From: Real Madrid
To: Arsenal

£42.4m

The England National Football Team

ENGLAND

The England national football team - controlled by The Football Association - played its first international match against Scotland in 1872. Along with the Scots, it's the joint-oldest team in the world. Since that 1-1 draw at The Oval cricket ground, which occasionally held football matches including the first FA Cup final, the country has followed the team wherever they go. England's greatest achievement came in 1966 when Sir Alf Ramsey led the Three Lions to the World Cup on home soil. There's been plenty of penalty shoot-out heartbreak since that historic day at Wembley Stadium, but no matter what the mood is leading up to a tournament, England always expects come a European Championship or World Cup. Many great players have pulled on the shirt, the captain's armband or scored numerous goals for England since 1872, with a number achieving legendary status.

Here we take a look at everything England - top goalscorers, managers, captains and other records.

Top goalscorers

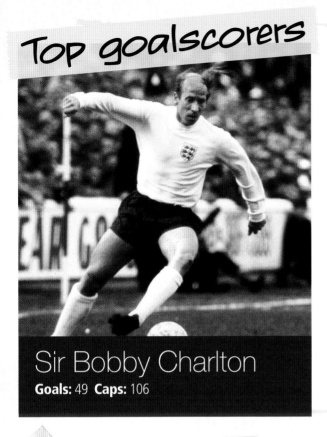

Sir Bobby Charlton
Goals: 49 **Caps:** 106

GARY LINEKER
Goals: 48 **Caps:** 80

JIMMY GREAVES
Goals: 44 **Caps:** 57

MICHAEL OWEN
Goals: 40 **Caps:** 89

WAYNE ROONEY
Goals: 38 **Caps:** 89

NAT LOFTHOUSE
Goals: 30 **Caps:** 33

ALAN SHEARER
Goals: 30 **Caps:** 63

TOM FINNEY
Goals: 30 **Caps:** 76

VIVIAN WOODWARD
Goals: 29 **Caps:** 23

FRANK LAMPARD
Goals: 29 **Caps:** 103

Managers

WALTER WINTERBOTTOM
1946-1962 139 games **Win percentage** 56.1%

ALF RAMSEY
1963-1974 113 games **Win percentage** 61.1%

JOE MERCER
1974 7 games **Win percentage** 42.9%

DON REVIE
1974-1977 29 games **Win percentage** 48.3%

RON GREENWOOD
1977-1982 55 games **Win percentage** 60%

BOBBY ROBSON
1982-1990 95 games **Win percentage** 49.5%

GRAHAM TAYLOR
1990-1993 38 games **Win percentage** 7.4%

TERRY VENABLES
1994-1996 23 games **Win percentage** 47.8%

GLENN HODDLE
1996-1999 28 games **Win percentage** 60.7%

HOWARD WILKINSON
1999 and 2000 2 games **Win percentage** 0%

KEVIN KEEGAN
1999-2000 18 games **Win percentage** 38.9%

PETER TAYLOR
2000 1 game **Win percentage** 0%

SVEN GORAN ERIKSSON
2001-2006 67 games **Win percentage** 59.7%

STEVE MCCLAREN
2006-2007 18 games **Win percentage** 50%

FABIO CAPELLO
2008-2012 42 games **Win percentage** 66.7%

STUART PEARCE
2012 1 game **Win percentage** 0%

ROY HODGSON
2012-present 25 games **Win percentage** 56%

Major Championships

WORLD CUP

1930 **Uruguay** - Did not enter

1934 **Italy** - Did not enter

1938 **France** - Did not enter

1950 **Brazil** - Group stages

1954 **Switzerland** - Quarter-finals

1958 **Sweden** - Group stages

1962 **Chile** - Quarter-finals

1970 **Mexico** - Quarter-finals

1974 **Germany** - Did not qualify

1978 **Argentina** - Did not qualify

1982 **Spain** - Second round

1986 **Mexico** - Quarter-finals

1990 **Italy** - Fourth place

1994 **United States** - Did not qualify

1998 **France** - Round of 16

2002 **Japan and South Korea** - Quarter-finals

2006 **Germany** - Quarter-finals

2010 **South Africa** - Round of 16

1966 England **Winners**

EUROPEAN CHAMPIONSHIP

1996 England Semi-finals

1960 France - Did not enter
1964 Spain - Did not enter
1968 Italy - Semi-finals
1972 Belgium - Did not qualify
1976 Yougoslavia - Did not qualify
1980 Sweden - Group stages
1984 France - Did not qualify
1988 Germany - Group stages
1992 Sweden - Group stages

2000 Belgium and Holland - Group stages
2004 Portugal - Quarter-finals
2008 Austria and Switzerland - Did not qualify
2012 Poland and Ukraine - Quarter-finals

Oldest player

STANLEY MATTHEWS

42 years, 103 days vs Denmark on May 15, 1957

Youngest player

THEO WALCOTT

17 years, 75 days vs Hungary on May 30, 2006

Biggest Victories

13-0 vs Ireland - February 18, 1882 - International friendly
13-2 vs Ireland - February 18, 1899 - British Home Championships
11-1 vs Austria - June 8, 1908 - International friendly
10-0 vs Portugal - May 25, 1947 - International friendly
10-0 vs USA - May 27, 1964 - International friendly
9-0 vs Ireland - March 9, 1895 - British Home Championships
9-1 vs Belgium - May 11, 1927 - World Cup qualifier
8-0 vs San Marino - March 22, 2013 - World Cup qualifier

Caps

50+ CLUB

Bryan Robson, Wayne Rooney, Michael Owen, Kenny Sansom, Gary Neville, Ray Wilkins, Rio Ferdinand, Gary Lineker, John Barnes, John Terry, Stuart Pearce, Terry Butcher, Tom Finney, David Seaman, Sol Campbell, Gordon Banks, Alan Ball, Martin Peters, Paul Scholes, Tony Adams, David Watson, Alan Shearer, Kevin Keegan, Ray Wilson, David Platt, Emile Heskey, Chris Waddle, Emlyn Hughes, Ray Clemence, Peter Beardsley, Des Walker, Phil Neville, Jimmy Greaves, Paul Gascoigne, Gareth Southgate, Johnny Haynes, Joe Cole, Jermain Defoe, Stanley Matthews, Glenn Hoddle, Gareth Barry, Paul Ince, David James, Trevor Francis, Teddy Sheringham, Glen Johnson, Phil Neal, James Milner

100+ CLUB

Frank Lampard,
Billy Wright,
Bobby Charlton,
Ashley Cole,
Bobby Moore,
Steven Gerrard,
David Beckham,
Peter Shilton

Captains

PRE-WAR

Charles Alcock, Claude Ashton, Norman Bailey, Charlie Bambridge, Sam Barkas, Jack Barker, Ernie Blenkinsop, Steve Bloomer, Alfred George Bower, Jack Brodie, Charlie Buchan, Tommy Cooper, George Cotterill, Bob Crompton, Stan Cullis, Arthur Cursham, Graham Doggart, Arthur Dunn, Willis Edwards, Frank Forman, Reginald Erskine Foster, John Goodall, Roy Goodall, Cunliffe Gosling, Arthur Grimsdell, Eddie Hapgood, Stanley Harris, Hubert Heron, Jack Hill, Bob Holmes, Jack Hudson, Jack Hunter, David Jack, Fred Kean, Arthur Knight, Tinsley Lindley, Ephraim Longworth, Thomas Lucas, Joe McCall, George Male, Billy Moon, Alexander Morten, Frank Moss, Ernest Needham, William Oakley, Cuthbert Ottaway, Basil Patchitt, Jesse Pennington, William Rawson, Gilbert Smith, Francis Sparks, Howard Spencer, Alf Strange, Henry Wace, Sam Wadsworth, Billy Walker, Arthur Walters, Percy Walters, George Wilson, Charles Wollaston, Vivian Woodward, Max Woosnam, Charles Wreford-Brown

POST-WAR

Tony Adams, Jimmy Armfield, Alan Ball, Gareth Barry, Peter Beardsley, David Beckham, Colin Bell, Terry Butcher, Sol Campbell, Mick Channon, Bobby Charlton, Trevor Cherry, Ronnie Clayton, Ray Clemence, Ashley Cole, Rio Ferdinand, Ron Flowers, Gerry Francis, Steven Gerrard, George Hardwick, Johnny Haynes, Emlyn Hughes, Paul Ince, Kevin Keegan, Martin Keown, Frank Lampard, Gary Lineker, Mick Mills, Bobby Moore, Alan Mullery, Phil Neal, Michael Owen, Scott Parker, Stuart Pearce, Martin Peters, David Platt, Alf Ramsey, Bryan Robson, Wayne Rooney, David Seaman, Alan Shearer, Peter Shilton, Frank Swift, John Terry, Phil Thompson, Dave Watson, Ray Wilkins, Billy Wright, Mark Wright

Undefeated Streaks

Every football team dreams of embarking on long unbeaten league runs because there is no worse feeling than losing, and there are a number of sides who have done exactly that. From Africa to Romania to Uruguay to Moldova, we take a look at some of the longest and most impressive sequences of results in world football.

ASEC Misosas (1989-1994) - 108 matches

Incredibly, the Ivorian giants went a colossal five years unbeaten under the guidance of Philippe Troussier. They lifted six successive Premier Division titles before finally being beaten 2-1 by SO Armee.

Steaua Bucharest
(1986-1989) - 106 matches

The Romanian side went an incredible three years unbeaten in domestic competitions, in which they grabbed three league titles and a European Cup after being Barcelona on penalties in Sevilla.

FC Sheriff (2006-2008) - 63 matches

Sheriff have long dominated Moldovan football but they reached a new milestone in the 2006-2007 season when they won the title by going through the whole season unbeaten before their arch-rivals FC Zimbru Chisinau finally ended the run.

Celtic (1915-1917) - 62 matches

Just under a century ago, the Scottish side went on a remarkable run under manager Willie Maley which saw them win three straight league titles, and even having to play two games in one day.

AC Milan (1991-1993) - 58 matches

Under Fabio Capello, who went on to manage England in 2008, AC Milan won the 1991-1992 Serie A title after going through the season unbeaten before their run came to an end against Parma in 1993.

Bayern Munich (2012-2014) - 53 matches

After going 18 months without tasting defeat in the Bundesliga and winning the 2013-14 title with seven games to spare, the German giants' fantastic run finally came to an end as they were beaten 1-0 by Augsburg.

FC Porto (2010-2012) - 55 matches

Under Jesualdo Ferreira, and then Andre Villas-Boas, Porto went on an incredible undefeated streak which saw them win the Primeira Liga title and the Europa League, before they were eventually beaten 3-1 by Gil Vicente.

Penarol (1966-1969) - 56 matches

One of Uruguay's most famous club sides embarked on a terrific run towards the end of the 1960s in which they won the Copa Libertadores, the Internacional Cup and two league titles before losing in September 1969.

Ajax (1994-1996) - 52 matches

With one of the best club sides ever seen, the team from the Dutch capital went an entire season unbeaten in both the Eredivisie and Champions League where they beat AC Milan in the final.

Juventus (2011-2012) - 49 matches

There must be something about the number 49. After reaching the same number of games that Arsenal did, Juventus were beaten 3-1 at home by Internazionale - their first ever defeat in the Juventus Stadium.

Arsenal (2003-2004) - 49 matches

Known as the Invincibles, Arsene Wenger's Arsenal won the 2003-2004 Premier League title by going through the 38-game season unbeaten - the first team to do so in more than a century before losing 2-0 to Manchester United.

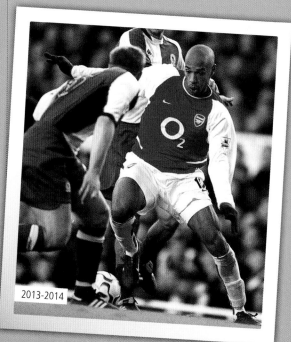

2013-2014

BIGGEST WINS

There can be no bigger humiliation for a footballer or team than a heavy defeat, and over the years there have been a number of examples of this all over the world. From club football to international football, here are some classic examples of the biggest and most famous winning margins in professional football.

England

England 13-0 Ireland
Date: February 18, 1882 **Competition:** International friendly

Newcastle United 13-0 Newport County
Date: October 5, 1946 **League:** Second Division

Stockport County 13-0 Halifax Town
Date: January 6, 1934 **League:** Third Division North

West Bromwich Albion 12-0 Darwen
Date: April 4, 1892 **League:** First Division

Nottingham Forest 12-0 Leicester Fosse
Date: March 21, 1909 **League:** First Division

Rest of the world

AS Adema 149-0 Stade Olympique L'Emyrne
Date: October 31, 2002 **Country:** Madagascar **Competition:** THB Champions League play-off

Arbroath 36-0 Bon Accord
Date: September 12, 1885 **Country:** Scotland **Competition:** Scottish Cup

Dundee Harp 35-0 Aberdeen Rangers
Date: September 12, 1885 **Country:** Scotland **Competition:** Scottish Cup

Australia 31-0 American Samoa
Date: April 11, 2011 **Country:** Australia **Competition:** World Cup qualifier

Villarreal 27-0 Navata
Date: July 19, 2009 **Country:** Spain **Competition:** Pre-season friendly

Most Successful
Managers

Every great team needs a great boss in order to win trophies. The men in the dugout need to be very good in order to succeed in the modern day game where time is not given due to the big financial rewards that can be gained through positive results. However, there are a number of managers down the years to have achieved major and multiple success. Here are the world's top 10 trophy laden chiefs.

Sir Alex Ferguson

49 TROPHIES

Fergie will always go down as one of the most respected managers in the history of the game. When he arrived at Old Trafford in 1986, he had already won ten trophies with Aberdeen, including two in European competitions, and his side dominated English football during the Premier League years. 13 league titles, five FA Cups and two Champions Leagues cover just some of the incredible 38 trophies he picked up as United manager before retiring in 2013.

Jock Stein 27 TROPHIES

Still widely recognised as the best ever coach in Scottish football history, Stein won ten league titles with Celtic. He had successful reigns at Hibernian and Dunfermline before he moved to Glasgow and became a club legend, picking up a total of 25 trophies, while fittingly he also led the Bhoys to their one and only European Cup success in 1967.

Ottmar Hitzfeld 25 TROPHIES

Regarded as one of the best coaches of his generation, Hitzfeld is one of the select few to lead two clubs - Bayern Munich and Borussia Dortmund - to Champions League success. His most successful spell came in charge of the former during two stints in which he won 14 trophies.

Giovanni Trappatoni 22 TROPHIES

The Trap is considered to be one of the most successful managers in the history of Serie A. His best spell came at Juventus between 1976 and 1986 when he won 14 trophies, including the European Cup in 1985. He has also had successful spells in Italy, Germany, Portugal and Austria, and managed the Republic of Ireland.

Walter Smith 22 TROPHIES

Smith will always be known as a Rangers legend and enjoyed great success during his two times at the helm of the Scottish giants during their dominance of the top flight with arch-rivals Celtic. He won a total of 21 trophies during those two spells, including ten league titles, and went on to help Scotland rise 70 places in the FIFA World Rankings.

Jose Mourinho 20 TROPHIES

The Special One has become one of the most successful managers in the modern era. The Portuguese boss won six trophies in two seasons in his first major job with FC Porto, and has since won league titles in England, Italy and Spain including a second Champions League title when lifting the trophy with Internazionale in 2010.

Bob Paisley 20 TROPHIES

A Liverpool legend, Paisley spent more than 50 years at the Merseyside club in different roles. Still the only boss to have won the European Cup on three separate occasions, the former long-term assistant to Bill Shankly was appointed as Reds manager in 1974 and guided the club to 20 trophies in nine seasons.

Marcello Lippi 18 TROPHIES

One of the most successful Italian managers of all time, Lippi enjoyed two hugely successful spells with Juventus in which he won five Serie A titles, the 1996 Champions League and 13 trophies altogether. His biggest achievement came in 2006 though, when he led Italy to World Cup glory in Germany after the Azzurri beat France on penalties.

Pep Guardiola 18 TROPHIES

Barcelona legend Guardiola was appointed manager in 2008. In his first season he led the club to the treble including the Champions League, and won a total of 14 trophies in his four seasons with the Spanish giants before winning the Bundesliga in his first term as Bayern Munich boss.

Brian Clough 16 TROPHIES

Charismatic and often controversial, Brian Clough will always be remembered as one of the best British managers. He won the First Division with Derby County before famously guiding Nottingham Forest to back-to-back European Cups in 1979 and 1980 - one of the greatest achievements in football history.

Honourable mention

Vicente del Bosque 10 TROPHIES

The Spaniard won two La Liga and two Champions League titles during his time with Real Madrid before leading one of the greatest national sides of all time, Spain, to World Cup and European Championship glory in 2010 and 2012 respectively.

Premier
CROWDS

The Premier League is often described as the best in the world and it is no surprise that stadiums are often near to full capacity for each and every game.

Of course, because of the Taylor Report that was published in 1991 following the Hillsborough disaster, all top flight stadiums must now be all-seater, meaning the average attendances in the modern day are significantly lower than the record attendances for each club when standing on terraces was the norm.

Manchester United hold both the highest average attendance in the modern day, and the record attendance for the current Premier League sides, while Southampton are the only club whose record attendance has come in the 21st century following their move to St. Mary's in 2001.

Here are the current 20 Premier League club's average and best crowds from the 2013-14 season, plus their club-record attendance.

Arsenal
Average: 60,013 **Best:** 60,071 **Record:** 73,295

Aston Villa
Average: 36,080 **Best:** 42,682 **Record:** 76,588

Burnley (Championship)
Average: 13,719 **Best:** 19,125 **Record:** 54,775 (FA Cup)

Chelsea
Average: 41,481 **Best:** 41,623 **Record:** 82,905

Crystal Palace
Average: 24,114 **Best:** 28,235 **Record:** 51,482

Everton
Average: 37,731 **Best:** 39,576 **Record:** 78,299

Hull City
Average: 24,076 **Best:** 24,940 **Record:** 55,019 (FA Cup)

Leicester City (Championship)
Average: 24,994 **Best:** 31,424 **Record:** 47,298 (FA Cup)

Liverpool
Average: 44,668 **Best:** 44,822 **Record:** 61,905

Manchester City
Average: 47,070 **Best:** 47,364 **Record:** 84,569 (FA Cup)

Manchester United
Average: 75,206 **Best:** 75,368 **Record:** 83,260

Newcastle United
Average: 50,395 **Best:** 52,280 **Record:** 68,386

QPR **(Championship)**
Average: 16,655 **Best:** 18,171 **Record:** 35,353 (FA Cup)

Southampton
Average: 30,147 **Best:** 31,659 **Record:** 32,363

Stoke City
Average: 26,137 **Best:** 27,429 **Record:** 51,380

Sunderland
Average: 40,585 **Best:** 46,313 **Record:** 75,118 (FA Cup)

Swansea City
Average: 20,406 **Best:** 20,769 **Record:** 32,796 (FA Cup)

Tottenham Hotspur
Average: 35,807 **Best:** 36,102 **Record:** 75,038 (FA Cup)

West Bromwich Albion
Average: 25,114 **Best:** 26,541 **Record:** 64,815 (FA Cup)

West Ham United
Average: 34,196 **Best:** 35,153 **Record:** 42,322

Top 5 British Attendances

Rangers - 118,567, Ibrox vs Celtic in Scottish Division One on January 2, 1939

Queen's Park - 95,722, Hampden Park vs Rangers in the Scottish Cup on January 18, 1930

Manchester City - 84,569, Maine Road vs Stoke City in the FA Cup sixth round on March 3, 1934

Manchester United - 83,260, Maine Road vs Arsenal in the First Division on January 17, 1948

Celtic - 83,000, Celtic Park vs Rangers in Scottish Division One on January 1, 1938

ONE CLUB MEN

It is often said that there is no loyalty in the game of football any more, but that isn't always the case. There have been a number of players over the years that have stuck with one club, including the following players, who have gained legendary status at their respective teams.

ANDRES INIESTA
BARCELONA
Position: Midfielder **Debut:** 2002

With Xavi and Carles Puyol moving on to new challenges in the summer of 2014, Iniesta is now Barcelona's longest serving player. The midfielder, who scored the winning goal in the 2010 World Cup final, has won 21 trophies at the Camp Nou and has made over 500 appearances since joining the academy aged 12 in 1996.

FRANCESCO TOTTI AS ROMA
Position: Forward **Debut:** 1993

The attacker made his debut for Roma at the age of 16 in 1993 and has gone on to make more than 700 appearances for the side from the Italian capital - a club record - as well as being their highest ever goalscorer too. He is often described as Roma's best ever player as well as being one of the finest players of his generation. Real Madrid tried to bring Totti to Spain on two separate occasions but he opted to stay with his home club.

RYAN GIGGS
MANCHESTER UNITED
Position: Midfielder **Debut:** 1991

Giggs has become a Red Devils legend. He made his United debut at the age of 17, has made more than 950 appearances for the club, and has won 13 Premier League titles and a Champions League winners medal. He also scored in every Premier League season up until the 2013-14 campaign, in which he was named interim manager for the final four matches of the season. Retired from playing that summer and is now assistant to boss Louis van Gaal at Old Trafford.

STEVEN GERRARD
LIVERPOOL
Position: Midfielder **Debut:** 1998

Gerrard has been described as one of the greatest English midfielders in history and it was clear to see he had amazing potential even when he made his debut for the Reds at the age of 18. He went on to succeed the previous Liverpool captain Sami Hyypia in 2003, and has made more than 650 appearances. His best moment came in 2005 when he inspired his side to win the Champions League just a year after rejecting the chance to join Chelsea.

JOHN TERRY
CHELSEA
Position: Defender **Debut:** 1998

A captain. A leader. A legend. Centre-back John Terry made his debut for Chelsea at the age of 17 and went on to captain the Blues, winning three Premier League titles as well as lifting the Champions League in 2012. He is the club's most successful captain and has made more than 600 appearances for the side from west London, scoring more than 50 goals.

IKER CASILLAS
REAL MADRID
Position: Goalkeeper **Debut:** 1998

Considered to be one of the finest goalkeepers of all time, Casillas is something of a legend at Real Madrid. He made his first-team debut for the club at the age of 17, and became the youngest stopper to appear in a Champions League final just four days after his 19th birthday in 2000. He has gone on to captain the team and make more than 650 appearances. The Spain skipper has remained at the club despite losing his place to Diego Lopez in January 2013.

DANIELE DE ROSSI AS ROMA
Position: Midfielder **Debut:** 2001

De Rossi has been recognised as an all-round midfielder throughout his career, due to his ability at tackling, passing and shooting. He is considered as one of Roma's stars and the heir to his team-mate Francesco Totti for the captain's armband. The Italy international made his debut for the club from the Italian capital at the age of 18 and has gone on to make more than 450 appearances despite being targeted by a number of other elite European clubs.

ROGERIO CENI
SAO PAOLO
Position: Goalkeeper **Debut:** 1993

Rogerio Ceni isn't your typical goalkeeper. He made his first appearance for the Brazilian club in 1993 and has gone on to make more than 1,100 appearances. That doesn't seem too strange. But the fact that he has also scored more than 100 goals in that time certainly is! From penalties to free-kicks, the stopper was recognised by the Guinness Book of World Records for the most appearances as a captain, the most goals in his position, and the record number of games for the same club.

WORLD'S MO$T VALUABLE CLUBS

Despite the majority of the world's football clubs struggling for money and being sold for a cut-price, there are an elite group that are worth staggering amounts of cash.

Financial experts believe that Real Madrid are the most valuable team on Earth, valued at a mind boggling £1.96 billion, while there are seven English Premier League clubs in the top 20.

So who else makes the list of the planet's most valuable clubs?

1 Real Madrid
Spain

£1.96bn

2
Manchester United
England
£1.88bn

3
Barcelona
Spain
£1.55bn

4
Arsenal
England
£792m

5
Bayern Munich
Germany
£779 m

6
AC Milan
Italy
£563 m

7
Chelsea
England
£536 m

8
Juventus
Italy
£413 m

9
Manchester City
England
£410 m

10
Liverpool
England
£388 m

11
Tottenham Hotspur
England
£310 m

12
Schalke 04
Germany
£296 m

13
Borussia Dortmund
Germany
£260 m

14
Internazionale
Italy
£239 m

15
Lyon
France
£219 m

16
Corinthians
Brazil
£213 m

17
Napoli
Italy
£196 m

18
Hamburg
Germany
£179 m

19
Marseille
France
£170 m

20
Newcastle United
England
£157 m

*figures before tax

HIGHEST PAID PLAYERS

Footballers' wages have been the topic of much debate over the years with many feeling they are paid over the top for simply kicking a ball around. However, our beautiful game is simply not just a game in the modern day era. The Premier League, Champions League and major international tournaments have transformed it into an entertainment business, driven by money.

The top players in the world are the ones that keep the fans coming back for more and the men that make the game the exciting box-office spectacle it is today.

So which players have the biggest annual salaries?

1 Lionel Messi
Barcelona

£31.1m

2

Cristiano Ronaldo
Real Madrid

£30.16m

3

Wayne Rooney
Manchester United

£15.5m

Gareth Bale
Real Madrid

£15.5m

5

Radamel Falcao
AS Monaco

£11.4m

6

Zlatan Ibrahimovic
Paris Saint-Germain

£11.3m

7

Sergio Aguero
Manchester City

£9.87m

8

Yaya Toure
Manchester City

£9.46m

9

Thiago Silva
Paris Saint-Germain

£9.8m

David Silva
Manchester City

£9.8m

HIGHEST
PAID
MANAG£RS

The world's top managers are not short of a bob or two when it comes to being paid, with many now earning a similar amount to the players that do the business for them on the pitch.

And with the amount of pressure they are put under, why shouldn't the men in the hot seat earn as much as the superstars they coach and look out for on a daily basis.

Some managers, like Jose Mourinho, are often worth the entrance money alone, with their passion and unique management style sometimes offering more entertainment than their players.

So which managers have the biggest annual salaries?

1 Jose Mourinho
Chelsea

£13.98m

2
Pep Guardiola
Bayern Munich

£12.34m

3
Roberto Mancini
Galatasaray

£11.51m

4
Carlo Ancelotti
Real Madrid

£11.10m

5
Fabio Capello
Russia national team

£9.87m

6
Marcello Lippi
Guangzhou Evergrande

£9.46m

7
Arsene Wenger
Arsenal

£7.89m

8
Roberto Di Matteo
unemployed - still being paid by Chelsea

£6.74m

9
Andre Villas-Boas
Zenit St Petersburg - still being paid by Tottenham Hotspur) -

£5.67m

10
Rafael Benitez
Napoli

£5.59m

*figures before tax

ENGLISH FOOTBALL
HALL OF FAME

The English Football Hall of Fame is currently based in the National Football Museum in Manchester. Its objective is to celebrate the achievements of a number of people in the English game. The most celebrated of inductees are the players, managers and teams selected by a panel of ex-players, pundits and football historians. Each year new members are added to the list with an induction for the new affiliates usually held in the Autumn.

2014 Inductees

TREVOR FRANCIS

Position: Striker
Date of birth: April 19, 1954
Place of birth: Plymouth, England
Clubs: Birmingham City, Detroit Express (loan), Nottingham Forest, Manchester City, Sampdoria, Atalanta, Rangers, Wollongong City, Queens Park Rangers, Sheffield Wednesday
International: England (52 caps, 12 goals)

A double European Cup winner with Nottingham Forest, Francis, who also won honours in America, Italy and Scotland became England's first £1m transfer when he moved from Birmingham to the City Ground in 1979.

HUGHIE GALLACHER

Position: Striker
Date of birth: February 2, 1903
Place of birth: Gateshead, England
Clubs: Queen of the South, Airdrieonians, Newcastle United, Chelsea, Derby County, Notts County, Grimsby Town, Gateshead
International: Scotland (20 caps, 23 goals)

Gallacher was a clinical striker, netting 463 times in 624 senior appearances. A skilful dribbler, the nippy forward was two footed and scored five goals in a game on four occasions. Only Kenny Dalglish and Denis Law have scored more international goals for Scotland.

MICHAEL OWEN

Position: Striker
Date of birth: December 14, 1979
Place of birth: Chester, England
Clubs: Liverpool, Real Madrid, Newcastle United, Manchester United, Stoke City
International: England (89 caps, 40 goals)

Owen burst on to the scene as an 18-year-old at the 1998 World Cup, scoring a wonderful solo goal against Argentina. Despite a career plagued by injury, the deadly finisher scored 40 times for England, played at five major international tournaments, scored 222 club career goals, won seven major honours and collected the Ballon d'Or in 2001.

JIMMY MCILROY

Position: Forward
Date of birth: October 25, 1931
Place of birth: Lambeg, England
Clubs: Glentoran, Burnley, Stoke City, Oldham Athletic
International: Northern Ireland (55 caps, 10 goals)

The Northern Irishman is regarded as one of Burnley's greatest ever players having won the First Division title in 1960 and reaching the 1962 FA Cup final. He scored 131 goals for the Clarets in 12 years at Turf Moor and represented Northern Ireland over 50 times.

PATRICK VIEIRA

Position: Midfielder
Date of birth: June 23, 1976
Place of birth: Dakar, Senegal
Clubs: Cannes, AC Milan, Arsenal, Juventus, Internazionale, Manchester City
International: France (107 caps, 6 goals)

One of the greatest midfielders the Premier League has ever seen, Vieira captained Arsenal to three top flight titles including the 2003-04 season which saw The Gunners go the whole domestic campaign unbeaten. The powerful Frenchman also won the 1998 World Cup, 2000 European Championship and five Serie A titles.

TEAMS

PRESTON NORTH END'S 'INVINCIBLES' OF 1888-89

The Lilywhites stormed to the first ever Football Leagut title, winning 18 and drawing four of their 22 games. They scored an incredible 74 goals and conceded just 15 to finish 11 points ahead of runners-up Aston Villa.

2013 Inductees

PLAYERS

Raich Carter
Eddie Gray
Cliff Jones
Matt Le Tissier
Mike Summerbee
Ray Wilkins

Peter Schmeichel also collected his Hall of Fame trophy, having missed his initial inauguration in 2003.

2011-2012 - Break for relocation of National Football Museum from Preston to Manchester.

2010 Inductees

PLAYERS

Charlie Buchan, Ian Callaghan
Ray Clemence, Johnny Giles
Francis Lee, Sir Alf Ramsey
Clem Stephenson

TEAM

England's 1966 World Cup winners

MANAGER

Henry Catterick

2009 Inductees

PLAYERS

Ossie Ardiles
Cliff Bastin
Sir Trevor Brooking
George Cohen
Frank McLintock

Len Shackleton
Teddy Sheringham
Frank Swift

MANAGERS

Malcolm Allison,
Joe Mercer

TEAMS

Manchester United's 'Busby Babes' of the 1950s
Manchester City of 1968-1970

2008 Special Awards – European Hall of Fame

PLAYERS

George Best
John Charles
Sir Bobby Charlton
Kenny Dalglish
Kevin Keegan
Neville Southall
Steven Gerrard

MANAGERS

Sir Matt Busby
Brian Clough
Sir Alex Ferguson

Bob Paisley
Sir Bobby Robson

TEAMS

Manchester United - 1968
Liverpool - 1978

ALL-TIME GREAT EUROPEAN FOOTBALLER

Michel Platini

2008 Inductees

PLAYERS

Jimmy Armfield
David Beckham
Steve Bloomer
Thierry Henry, Emlyn Hughes
Paul Scholes, Ray Wilson

MANAGER

Bertie Mee

2007 Inductees

PLAYERS
Peter Beardsley
Dennis Bergkamp
Glenn Hoddle
Mark Hughes
Billy Meredith
Graeme Souness
Nobby Stiles

MANAGER
Terry Venables

2006 Inductees

PLAYERS
Liam Brady
Alan Hansen
Roger Hunt
Jackie Milburn
Martin Peters
Ian Rush
Gianfranco Zola

MANAGERS
Ron Greenwood
Arsène Wenger

2005 Inductees

PLAYERS
John Barnes
Colin Bell
Jack Charlton
Ryan Giggs
Alex James
Bert Trautmann
Ian Wright

MANAGERS
Howard Kendall
Sir Walter Winterbottom

2004 Inductees

PLAYERS
Tony Adams
Viv Anderson
Billy Bremner
Sir Geoff Hurst
Roy Keane
Wilf Mannion
Alan Shearer

MANAGERS
Dario Gradi
Don Revie

2003 Inductees

PLAYERS
Alan Ball
Danny Blanchflower
Pat Jennings

Tommy Lawton
Gary Lineker
Stan Mortensen
Peter Schmeichel
Arthur Wharton

MANAGERS
Herbert Chapman
Stan Cullis
Bill Nicholson
Sir Bobby Robson

2002 Inaugural Inductees

PLAYERS
Gordon Banks
George Best
Eric Cantona
John Charles
Sir Bobby Charlton

Kenny Dalglish
William "Dixie" Dean
Peter Doherty
Duncan Edwards
Sir Tom Finney
Paul Gascoigne
Jimmy Greaves
Johnny Haynes
Kevin Keegan
Denis Law
Nat Lofthouse
Dave Mackay
Sir Stanley Matthews
Bobby Moore
Bryan Robson
Peter Shilton
Billy Wright

MANAGERS
Sir Matt Busby
Brian Clough
Sir Alex Ferguson
Bob Paisley
Sir Alf Ramsey
Bill Shankly

Shoot's
Superstars

Today's top players are idolised around the world. There are a whole host of superstars showcasing their talents on a weekly basis - far too many to list here. So here's a selection of what Shoot consider to be the planet's elite players.

Iker Casillas

Position: Goalkeeper
Birth date: May 20, 1981
Birth place: Mostoles, Spain
Height: 1.85m (6ft 1in)
Clubs: Real Madrid
International: Spain
Began career: 1998

It's a fact: At the age of 33, Casillas has played over 675 games for Real Madrid having made his senior debut at the age of 18. He also captained Spain to three major tournaments titles - Euro 2008, 2012 and the 2010 World Cup.

Manuel Neuer

Position: Goalkeeper
Birth date: March 27, 1986
Birth place: Gelsenkirchen, West Germany
Height: 1.93m (6ft 4in)
Clubs: Schalke 04, Bayern Munich
International: Germany
Began career: 2004

It's a fact: Neuer was named as the 2013 World Goalkeeper of the Year. His £18.1m move to Bayern in 2009 made him the second most expensive stopper of all time behind Italy's Gianluigi Buffon.

Petr Cech

Position: Goalkeeper
Birth date: May 20, 1982
Birth place: Plzen, Czechoslovakia
Height: 1.96m (6ft 5in)
Clubs: Chmel Blsany, Sparta Prague, Rennes, Chelsea
International: Czech Republic
Began career: 1999

It's a fact: Cech has won the Premier League, FA Cup, League Cup, Community Shield, Champions League and Europa League with Chelsea. He has also won the Premier League Golden Glove (for most clean sheets) in 2004-05, 2009-10 and 2013-14.

Thiago Silva

Position: Defender
Birth date: September 22, 1984
Birth place: Rio de Janeiro, Brazil
Height: 1.83m (6ft 0in)
Clubs: RS Futebol, Juventude, FC Porto, Dynamo Moscow, Fluminense, AC Milan, Paris Saint-Germain
International: Brazil
Began career: 2003

It's a fact: Brazil's current captain has won league titles in Brazil, Italy and France. He reportedly cost PSG in the region of £35.5m in July 2012.

Jordi Alba

Position: Defender
Birth date: March 21, 1989
Birth place: L'Hospitalet, Spain
Height: 1.70m (5ft 7in)
Clubs: Valencia, Gimnastic (loan), Barcelona
International: Spain
Began career: 2007

It's a fact: Barcelona released Alba as a 16-year-old before re-signing him from Valencia for £11.5m. He scored in Spain's 4-0 Euro 2012 final victory against Italy.

Philipp Lahm

Position: Defender
Birth date: November 11, 1983
Birth place: Munich, Germany
Height: 1.70m (5ft 7in)
Clubs: Bayern Munich, VfB Stuttgart (loan)
International: Germany
Began career: 2001

It's a fact: Lahm can play on both sides of defence and in midfield. He scored the opening goal of the 2006 World Cup and has won six Bundesliga titles.

Andres Iniesta

Position: Midfielder
Birth date: May 11, 1984
Birth place: Fuentealbilla, Spain
Height: 1.70m (5ft 7in)
Clubs: Barcelona
International: Spain
Began career: 2001

It's a fact: Iniesta scored the winner in the 2010 World Cup final and was voted Euro 2012 Player of the Tournament. He's also won over 20 trophies with Barcelona including three Champions League titles.

Yaya Toure

Position: Midfielder
Birth date: May 13, 1983
Birth place: Bouake, Ivory Coast
Height: 1.91m (6ft 3in)
Clubs: Beveren, Metalurh Donetsk, Olympiacos, Monaco, Barcelona, Manchester City
International: Ivory Coast
Began career: 2001

It's a fact: In 2013, Toure became the first player to be named the Confederation of African Football Footballer of the Year three years in a row. He's won league titles in four different countries (Ivory Coast, Greece, Spain, England).

Franck Ribery

Position: Midfielder
Birth date: April 7, 1983
Birth place: Boulogne-sur-Mer, France
Height: 1.70m (5ft 7in)
Clubs: Boulogne, Ales, Stade Brestois, Metz, Galatasaray, Marseille, Bayern Munich
International: France
Began career: 2000

It's a fact: Ribery finished third, behind Cristiano Ronaldo and Lionel Messi, for the 2013 Ballon d'Or. He was also named as UEFA's Best Player in Europe for the 2012-13 season, as Bayern Munich won a historic quadruple.

Neymar

Position: Forward
Birth date: February 5, 1992
Birth place: Mogi das Cruzes, Brazil
Height: 1.75m (5ft 9in)
Clubs: Santos, Barcelona
International: Brazil
Began career: 2009

It's a fact: Neymar scored on his Brazil debut against the United States at the age of 18. He struck his first goal for Barcelona against Atletico Madrid in the 2012 Spanish Super Cup.

Cristiano Ronaldo

Position: Forward
Birth date: February 5, 1995
Birth place: Madeira, Portugal
Height: 1.85m (6ft 1in)
Clubs: Sporting Lisbon, Manchester United, Real Madrid
International: Portugal
Began career: 2002

It's a fact: Ronaldo's £80m transfer from Manchester United to Real Madrid was a world record prior to Gareth Bale's £85m move to the same club. He has captained Portugal at three major tournaments, won two Ballon d'Or trophies and hit 250 Madrid goals in just 243 games.

Lionel Messi

Position: Forward
Birth date: June 24, 1987
Birth place: Rosario, Argentina
Height: 1.69 (5ft 7in)
Clubs: Barcelona
International: Argentina
Began career: 2004

It's a fact: Messi is the only player to have won the Ballon d'Or four times. He scored the most goals (91) in a calendar year in 2012, has won 21 trophies with Barcelona and is the club's record scorer with over 350 goals.

Luis Suarez

Position: Forward
Birth date: January 24, 1987
Birth place: Salto, Uruguay
Height: 1.81m (5ft 11in)
Clubs: Nacional, Groningen, Ajax, Liverpool
International: Uruguay
Began career: 2005

It's a fact: Suarez was named the 2013-14 PFA Player of the Year after scoring over 30 Premier League goals for Liverpool. He became his country's record scorer when he struck his 35th Uruguay goal against Tahiti at the 2013 Confederations Cup.

Zlatan Ibrahimovic

Position: Striker
Birth date: October 3, 1981
Birth place: Malmo, Sweden
Height: 1.95m (6ft 5in)
Clubs: Malmo FF, Ajax, Juventus, Internazionale, Barcelona, Milan, Paris Saint-Germain
International: Sweden
Began career: 1999

It's a fact: Ibrahimovic is the most expensive player in football history with his combined transfer fees totalling £133.2m. He has won a league title in four of the five countries he's played in and has scored over 20 goals in each of the last seven seasons.

Sergio Aguero

Position: Striker
Birth date: June 2, 1988
Birth place: Buenos Aires, Argentina
Height: 1.73m (5ft 8in)
Clubs: Independiente, Atletico Madrid, Manchester City
International: Argentina
Began career: 2003

It's a fact: Aguero cost Manchester City £38m in 2011. He scored 30 goals in his debut season in England including the famous last minute Premier League title clincher against QPR. He has played at two World Cups and won a gold medal at the 2008 Beijing Olympic Games with Argentina.

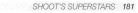

Shoot's
Young Stars

S ome players take time to establish themselves at the top of the game but there are many talented individuals who hit the ground running from an early age. It's an exciting sight watching a fearless, talented youngster take the game to their more experienced fellow professionals. Here is Shoot's selection of the best young players in the world.

Maksym Koval

Position: Goalkeeper
Birth date: December 9, 1992
Birth place: Zaporizhya, Ukraine
Height: 1.88m (6ft 2in)
Clubs: Metalurh Zaporizhya, Dynamo Kiev
International: Ukraine
Began career: 2008

It's a fact: Koval made his international debut at the age of 20 as a second half substitute before being included in Ukraine's squad for Euro 2012.

Marc-Andre Ter Stegen

Position: Goalkeeper
Birth date: April 30, 1992
Birth place: Monchengladbach, Germany
Height: 1.89m (6ft 2in)
Clubs: Borussia Monchengladbach, Barcelona
International: Germany
Began career: 2009

It's a fact: At the age of 19, the German kept four clean sheets in the last five Bundesliga games to help Monchengladbach survive relegation via the play-offs.

Thibaut Courtois

Position: Goalkeeper
Birth date: May 11, 1992
Birth place: Bree, Belgium
Height: 1.99m (6ft 6in)
Clubs: Genk, Chelsea, Atletico Madrid (loan)
International: Belgium
Began career: 2009

It's a fact: Courtois knocked his parent club Chelsea out of the 2013-14 Champions League while on loan at Atletico Madrid.

Luke Shaw

Position: Defender
Birth date: July 12, 1995
Birth place: Kingston upon Thames, England
Height: 1.85m (6ft 1in)
Clubs: Southampton
International: England
Began career: 2012

It's a fact: Shaw was named in the 2013-14 PFA Team of the Year in a season which saw him become England's 12th youngest ever player.

David Alaba

Position: Defender
Birth date: June 24, 1992
Birth place: Vienna, Austria
Height: 1.80m (5ft 11in)
Clubs: Austria Wien II, Bayern Munich, 1899 Hoffenheim (loan)
International: Austria
Began career: 2007

It's a fact: Alaba is Austria's youngster ever player and was named his country's Footballer of the Year in 2011, 2012 and 2013.

Raphael Varane

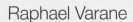

Position: Defender
Birth date: April 25, 1993
Birth place: Lille, France
Height: 1.91m (6ft 3in)
Clubs: Lens, Real Madrid
International: France
Began career: 2010

It's a fact: Varane played for Lille's first-team for less than a year before making an £8m move to Real Madrid.

Paul Pogba

Position: Midfielder
Birth date: March 15, 1993
Birth place: Lagny-sur-Marne, France
Height: 1.86m (6ft 1in)
Clubs: Manchester United, Juventus
International: France
Began career: 2011

It's a fact: Pogba won consecutive Serie A titles and won his first France cap in his first two seasons with Juventus.

Alex Oxlade-Chamberlain

Position: Midfielder
Birth date: August 15, 1993
Birth place: Portsmouth, England
Height: 1.80m (5ft 11in)
Clubs: Southampton, Arsenal
International: England
Began career: 2010

It's a fact: In 2012, Chamberlain became the second youngest player to represent England at the European Championship finals.

Adnan Januzaj

Position: Midfielder
Birth date: February 5, 1995
Birth place: Brussels, Belgium
Height: 1.80m (5ft 11in)
Clubs: Manchester United
International: Belgium
Began career: 2013

It's a fact: Januzaj opted to play for his birth country Belgium but was also eligible to play for Albania, Kosovo and England.

Julian Draxler

Position: Midfielder
Birth date: September 20, 1993
Birth place: Gladbeck, Germany
Height: 1.87m (6ft 1in)
Clubs: Schalke 04
International: Germany
Began career: 2011

It's a fact: Draxler became the second youngster player to ever start a Bundesliga game in January 2011.

Mario Gotze

Position: Midfielder
Birth date: June 3, 1992
Birth place: Memmingen, Germany
Height: 1.76m (5ft 9in)
Clubs: Borussia Dortmund, Bayern Munich
International: Germany
Began career: 2009

It's a fact: Gotze became the second most expensive German player of all time when he made his £31.5m to Bayern Munich.

Jese Rodriguez

Position: Winger
Birth date: February 26, 1993
Birth place: Las Palmas, Spain
Height: 1.78m (5ft 10in)
Clubs: Real Madrid
International: Spain
Began career: 2011

It's a fact: Jese replaced Cristiano Ronaldo for his La Liga debut in March 2012 and scored his first competitive goal against Barcelona in October 2013.

Lazar Markovic

Position: Winger
Birth date: March 2, 1994
Birth place: Cacak, FR Yugoslavia
Height: 1.75m (5ft 9in)
Clubs: Partizan, Benfica
International: Serbia
Began career: 2011

It's a fact: Markovic made 43 appearances in his debut season for Benfica as he helped the club win their first league title in four years.

Viktor Fischer

Position: Forward
Birth date: June 9, 1994
Birth place: Aarhus, Denmark
Height: 1.80m (5ft 11in)
Clubs: Ajax
International: Denmark
Began career: 2012

It's a fact: Fischer made his Champions League debut at the age of 18 in Ajax's group match at Manchester City in 2012.

Romelu Lukaku

Position: Striker
Birth date: May 13, 1993
Birth place: Antwerp, Belgium
Height: 1.90m (6ft 3in)
Clubs: Anderlecht, Chelsea, West Bromwich Albion (loan), Everton (loan)
International: Belgium
Began career: 2009

It's a fact: Lukaku made his Belgium debut at the age of 16, the same year he struck 19 goals in his first full season for Anderlecht.

Shoot's
Legends

There have been many great players to grace a football pitch. Some have earned personal recognition through consistent world-class performances, while others are known for being part of successful teams. Here we look at Shoot's selection of players who have earned the right to be called legends. This list only involves players to have retired from the game without winning the Ballon d'Or.

Oliver Kahn

Position: Goalkeeper
Birth date: June 15, 1969
Birth place: Karlsruhe, West Germany
Height: 1.88m (6ft 2in)
Clubs: Karlsruher SC, Bayern Munich
International: Germany (86 caps)
Began career: 1987

It's a fact: Khan became the first and only goalkeeper in history to win the Golden Ball as Germany reached the 2002 World Cup final.

Peter Schmeichel

Position: Goalkeeper
Birth date: November 18, 1963
Birth place: Gladsaxe, Denmark
Height: 1.91m (6ft 3in)
Clubs: Gladsaxe Hero, Hvidovre, Brondby, Manchester United, Sporting CP, Aston Villa, Manchester City
International: Denmark (129 caps, 1 goal)
Began career: 1981

It's a fact: Schmeichel won the 1992 European Championship with Denmark and scored 10 goals throughout his 22-year career.

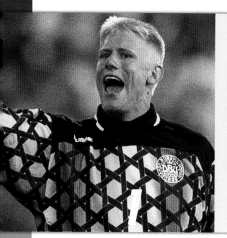

Dino Zoff

Position: Goalkeeper
Birth date: February 28, 1942
Birth place: Mariano del Friuli, Italy
Height: 1.85m (6ft 1in)
Clubs: Udinese, Mantova, Napoli, Juventus
International: Italy (112 caps)
Began career: 1961

It's a fact: Zoff is the oldest player in history to have won a World Cup having won the 1982 tournament at the age of 40.

Bobby Moore

Position: Defender
Birth date: April 12, 1941
Birth place: Barking, England
Height: 1.88m (6ft 2in)
Clubs: West Ham United, Fulham, San Antonio Thunder, Seattle Sounders, Herning Fremad
International: England (108 caps, 2 goals)
Began career: 1958

It's a fact: Moore captained England to the 1966 World Cup on home soil and won 108 caps in all for his country.

Cafu

Position: Defender
Birth date: June 7, 1970
Birth place: Sao Paulo, Brazil
Height: 1.76m (5ft 9in)
Clubs: Sao Paulo, Real Zaragoza, Juventude, Palmeiras, Roma, AC Milan
International: Brazil (142 caps, 5 goals)
Began career: 1990

It's a fact: Cafu won two World Cups (1994 and 2002) with Brazil and is his country's record caps holder with 142.

Paolo Maldini

Position: Defender
Birth date: June 26, 1968
Birth place: Milan, Italy
Height: 1.86m (6ft 1in)
Clubs: AC Milan
International: Italy (126 caps, 7 goals)
Began career: 1985

It's a fact: Maldini won seven Serie A titles and five European Cups during a 902-game career with Milan.

Zico

Position: Midfielder
Birth date: March 3, 1953
Birth place: Rio de Janeiro, Brazil
Height: 1.72m (5ft 7in)
Clubs: Flamengo, Udinese, Kashima Antlers
International: Brazil (71 caps, 48 goals)
Began career: 1971

It's a fact: Zico represented Brazil at three World Cups and is his country's fourth highest scorer with 48 goals in 71 caps.

Roy Keane

Position: Midfielder
Birth date: August 10, 1971
Birth place: Cork, Ireland
Height: 1.78m (5ft 10in)
Clubs: Cobh Ramblers, Nottingham Forest, Manchester United, Celtic
International: Republic of Ireland (67 caps, 9 goals)
Began career: 1989

It's a fact: Keane won 17 trophies including a Champions League, FA Cup, and Premier League treble in 1999, in 13 years with Manchester United.

Frank Rijkaard

Position: Midfielder
Birth date: September 30, 1962
Birth place: Amsterdam, Holland
Height: 1.90m (6ft 3in)
Clubs: Ajax, Sporting CP, Real Zaragoza (loan), Milan
International: Holland (73 caps, 10 goals)
Began career: 1980

It's a fact: Rijkaard helped Holland win the 1988 European Championship and was named in the Team of the Tournament.

Garrincha

Position: Winger
Birth date: October 28, 1933
Birth place: Pau Grande, Brazil
Height: 1.69m (5ft 7in)
Clubs: Botafogo, Corinthians, Portuguesa Carioca, Atletico Junior, Flamengo, Olaria
International: Brazil (50 caps, 12 goals)
Began career: 1953

It's a fact: Garrincha was born with bent legs but it didn't stop him winning two World Cups (1958 and 1962) with Brazil.

Francisco Gento

Position: Winger
Birth date: October 21, 1933
Birth place: Guarnizo, Spain
Height: 1.71m (5ft 6in)
Clubs: Racing Santander, Real Madrid
International: Spain (43 caps, 5 goals)
Began career: 1952

It's a fact: Gento was part of the famous Real Madrid side that won five European Cups in a row from 1956 to 1960.

Ferenc Puskas

Position: Forward
Birth date: April 2, 1927
Birth place: Budapest, Hungary
Height: 1.72m (5ft 8in)
Clubs: Budapest Honved, Real Madrid
International: Hungary (85 caps, 84 goals), Spain (4 caps)
Began career: 1943

It's a fact: Puskas scored 84 goals in 85 games for Hungary and 616 times in 620 club career matches.

Pele

Position: Forward
Birth date: October 21, 1940
Birth place: Tres Coracoes, Brazil
Height: 1.73m (5ft 8in)
Clubs: Santos, New York Cosmos
International: Brazil (92 caps, 77 goals)
Began career: 1956

It's a fact: Pele is the only man to have won three World Cups, with the first victory coming as a 17-year-old in 1958.

Diego Maradona

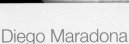

Position: Forward
Birth date: October 30, 1960
Birth place: Buenos Aires, Argentina
Height: 1.65m (5ft 5in)
Clubs: Argentinos Juniors, Boca Juniors, Barcelona, Napoli, Sevilla, Newell's Old Boys, Boca Juniors
International: Argentina (91 caps, 34 goals)
Began career: 1976

It's a fact: Maradona captained Argentina to the 1986 World Cup and was bought for a world record transfer fee twice in his career.

Hugo Sanchez

Position: Striker
Birth date: July 11, 1958
Birth place: Mexico City, Mexico
Height: 1.75m (5ft 9in)
Clubs: UNAM, San Diego Sockers (loan), Atletico Madrid, Real Madrid, America, Reyo Vallecano, Atlante, Linz, Dallas Burn, Celaya
International: Mexico (58 caps, 29 goals)
Began career: 1976

It's a fact: Sanchez's 207 goals in 283 Real Madrid games helped the club win five consecutive La Liga titles from 1986 to 1990.

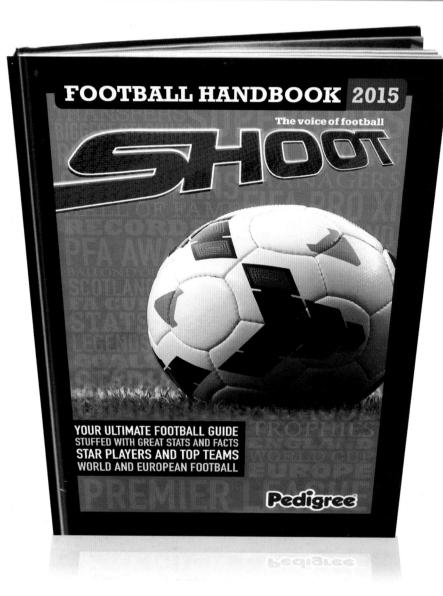